The History

of the

Borough of Reigate Fire Brigade

NEVER SHALL
WONNE NE NEVER

by
Alan Moore
and
Derek Chinery

This book about the Borough Brigade is dedicated to
Reigate Fire Fighters past and present,
with some of whom I spent a good part
of my fire service career.
Derek Chinery June 2003

Front Cover: The Fire Brigades of Surrey Preservation Trust
has undertaken all reasonable efforts to identify the artist and
origin of the picture but has been unsuccessful, therefore the
Trust has used the picture in good faith and would welcome
any information on its history.

Research and text
by Alan Moore

Photographs captions and other material
by Derek Chinery

First published 2003
Copyright Fire Brigades of Surrey Preservation Trust

Designed and Printed by
Litho Techniques (Kenley) Ltd

Published by Fire Brigades of Surrey Preservation Trust
(Registered charity No 297162)

Captain Fred Legg

The Fireman

The Fireman's life is a gallant life
All dangers will he brave,

To rescue mother, father and child
From death and fiery grave.

Oh! Never cares he if the perishing be
Of high or lowly grade,

Unflinching he goes where the red heat glows,
Their noble deed record.
For the dangers that they undergo,
May heaven be their reward.

Sponsored by Reigate & Banstead
Borough Council

CONTENTS

PREFACE

The purpose of this book is to record that which, to the best of my knowledge, has not been fully recorded before. It is obvious that not everything can be here, far from it, but hopefully there is enough to make it a fairly full account of the Fire Brigades of the Borough of Reigate from their inception to their centralisation as a single Brigade at St David's, Reigate, in the mid-1950s. As with most historical information, the facts have to be searched out from wherever they can be found and this is, therefore, a history compiled from various printed sources and first hand accounts.

I would point out that I have little direct knowledge of the Fire Service generally, having never served in it, so write purely as an interested (and definitely amateur) historian, and not at all as knowledgeable fireman, nor as an especially qualified social observer. This might make some aspects of this history easier for fellow layman to read, while perhaps less interesting for those aficionados who require the full technical detail which I am unqualified and unable to give. Any information appearing to contravene this basic fact is derived from the knowledge and guidance of experts Ron Shettle and Derek Chinery.

Additional local history information places events more firmly in the context of the times in which they occurred. The definition of the Borough of Reigate, as far as this history is concerned, is the firstly the old Manor of Reigate as it was from Norman times, and then the Borough as it became just after the middle of the last century at the time of Incorporation. It comprises Redhill and Reigate, with the inclusion of South Park, Earlswood, Meadvale, and later Merstham and Gatton.

Events make news but people make history, and many of their names have made it through the years to appear on these pages. All too often chance decides who gets remembered and who gets forgotten, so let none of us forget those Borough of Reigate firemen and firewomen who made the history on the following pages.

AJM

Chapter One
The Early Years

Early Fire Fighting in England

Fire, when confined to a manageable and useful size, is a tool of enormous benefit, and it is undeniable that without its properties man would not have been able to progress and develop his skills and knowledge as he has. Fire can, however, all too easily escape its man-made confines to become a dangerously destructive force, a hazard that has always been rightly feared. When this happens, other forces, knowledge and skills, as well as other tools are needed to deal with it.

Very early man would have had no defence against fire, fleeing before brush or forest fires that may have occurred in his vicinity. The Romans, however, recognised the fact that the use of fire and the proximity of houses made a fire fighting force a necessary precaution and had groups of slaves to fight fires. Known as *Familia Publica* they were not an efficient force and were replaced by a *Corps of Vigiles* who were to protect Rome for 500 years. The tools at their disposal included blankets, probably wetted and hung on walls adjacent to a fire to protect from radiated heat, ladders, buckets, long poles with hooks for dragging off burning material, and axes, these latter presumably for gaining access to premises for the purpose of continuing the fight within. In addition it is also possible that they had hand 'squirts' for projecting water onto a fire, water pumps with bronze pistons and cylinders for expelling water to a height, parts of which have been found in some Roman cities, including Silchester, Hampshire. Other than this latter find there is little evidence of the *Vigiles* activity in Roman Britain.

When the Romans left this country their place was taken by the Saxon invaders who settled the land as farmers. They ignored the remains of the Roman cities and lived in rural conditions in scattered wooden and thatched dwellings. Because of the ease with which a wooden building could be replaced using readily available materials, and the general isolation of buildings, there was little danger from fire other than to that single building, and fire fighting methods were generally neglected for four hundred years.

It was not until the Danish invasions that the importance of provisioned stockaded settlements caused Alfred the Great to create a number of such sites. These were the forerunners of English towns and cities wherein houses were close enough together for the risk of fire in one spreading to others. From this time it once again became necessary to take precautions against fire and put in place measures to fight it. Bells were rung at night to signal a time to extinguish all flames - the curfew, as it became known - and the ringing of bells at other times was a signal to warn of fires and alert the populace to the need to deal with them. Once more there were buckets, poles with hooks, ladders and water supplies available.

History tells us how ineffective these measures were against man's old enemy. For century after century disastrous fires that burnt for days and destroyed great swathes of English cities from Chichester to Carlisle occurred. London burnt several times, once in 1212 with an estimated 3,000 fatalities. This was known as the Great Fire until the fire of 1666 that is generally better known as the Great Fire of London, in which 4,000 homes and 300 streets were destroyed. Many such fires were started accidentally, begun by cooking fires usually, but fire was a tool of warfare and of revenge also.

Houses of stone were less likely to burn but were generally afforded only by the rich, the poor continuing to live in wooden thatched accommodation that was a conflagration waiting to happen. Flammable material such as wood for basic construction and straw for roof thatching, was readily used extensively in crowded conditions. With candles and oil as the only form of illumination, and open grate fires often without chimneys, it is little wonder that there were ever places that at some time were not devastated. In areas where stone was more easily available as a building material fewer major conflagrations occurred.

Even so, fire fighting methods remained primitive for hundreds of years. The local sweep might have been relied upon to extinguish chimney fires, and smothering a small fire with earth or sand, or beating a more widespread one with sticks or besoms, was sometimes effective. Dousing fire with water was better still, but water, especially under pressure, was not always readily to hand, and in the case of large fires that were beyond the capabilities of one or two individuals to deal with organised effort was required. In villages and towns, fire fighting materials began to be kept in a centralised location, like a church or Town Hall, to deal with general fires, and the assistance of those neighbours who were not working too far away in the fields was relied upon. Two men could carry a large bucket or barrel of water to create a supply for bucket chains when a pond or river was not near enough. The long pole hooks for dragging burning material, even whole, blazing roofs down, were mounted on wheels and hitched to horses for extra reach and pulling power.

The law was used to punish those who created conditions where property and life might be endangered by fire. The storage of flammable materials was regulated, wooden chimneys (difficult to believe they were actually used) were outlawed, and the provision of fire fighting equipment as already outlined, was made compulsory. In some towns it was the duty of the local brewer to turn up at any fire with his dray loaded with barrels of water, in others for every citizen to have a bucket ready to be used in the case of fire at any point in the town.

More organised and efficient methods than these had to wait until the sixteenth century when there came the re-invention of the fire 'squirt', syringes that were sometimes mounted on wheels and were the forerunners of the cylinder pumps of the following century. These early mechanical devices and the arrival of the first flexible hose in 1672 led to the hand pumped engine that was patented in 1700 with a design that produced a basis for other engine makers for over a hundred years.

Explosives were sometimes used in order to quell, or at least limit the spread of large fires. This method was employed in the already referred to 1666 Great Fire of London. Houses were blown up to stop the fire's progress, a successful manoeuvre after three days of conflagration in which there was so much destruction. This fire brought forward the concept of financial fire risk cover, and with it the development of private fire fighting bodies of men. These were the forerunners of the present-day brigades and they created the need for the development and expansion of the methods and equipment adopted as the tools of their trade.

Pre-1800-1809 - Fire Fighting Methods in Reigate

Reigate town was fortunate to have a ready head of water at its disposal in the shape of the moat that once protected the castle. Built in the 1100s it was tapped at an unknown date by a pipe that led down to a building called 'the Cage', which was the local detention centre.

An early prison, approached from the Crown Steps, had stood in a yard behind Glover's shop, itself situated on the north side of the High Street just east of the current Old Town Hall. This was torn down well before 1800 and its successor built almost in the centre of the present junction of Bell Street, Church Street and the High Street, and known also as the Clock House due to the cupola and clock that adorned its roof. There was, therefore, a reliable water source of considerable volume at the centre of the town right from where it could have been rapidly be transported to any nearby burning building.

The pipes would probably been made of hollowed logs of a dense wood such as elm. Each one would have been tapered at one end to fit into the end of the next and treated with pitch, especially at the joints, to prevent leakage, and may have been made stronger with the addition of metal bands. Some kind of stopcock would have been needed at the cage end and would have had to have been of substantial build to prevent leakage, as the head of water would have produced a fairly considerable pressure. Other towns had similar systems of piping or channelling water to convenient points from local supplies.

The cage in the Market Square was superseded as a prison by a new cage built in Mint Yard in 1801, the name of which was changed to Cage Yard. This building is now the Cage Wine Bar. The old cage seems to have survived until 1811, when the clock and cupola were removed and placed on top of the Old Town Hall. The part of the moat to which the pipe was connected was destroyed when a tunnel and its approaches were cut through under the Castle Grounds in around 1823, so if the water supply remained after the demise of the cage it certainly dried up following this later event. [4] There is a report of a public letter having been written by a Mr William Bryant about the loss of the water supply. This letter has not been seen but he may have been protesting about the increased danger to the town.

The Manor of Reigate
Before we proceed any further a brief explanation of the structure of the Borough under the old Norman manorial system that existed before the current council system of local government came into being should be made.

The Reigate area was, for reasons of administration, divided into distinct parts. First of all there was the Old Borough, which was the 400 acres of Reigate town itself. Around it was the Foreign, the 6000 acres of which comprised all of the rest of the Manor. The Foreign was itself divided into the five boroughs of Colley, Santon, Linkfield and Hooley. Together with the Old Borough they formed the whole of the Manor of Reigate. Redhill did not come into being until the 1840s.

Overlaid on the Manor was the Parish. Although not exactly the same as the Manor it was nevertheless an area similar to its shape and size, having roughly corresponding boundaries with St Mary Magdalene's church at its centre. The Manor and the Parish were intertwined quite strongly. Each Borough had its own administrative body to tend to its affairs. In addition the Parish had two administrative bodies of its own, called Vestries, one for the Old Borough and one for the Foreign. These administered the day-to-day affairs of the Parish and were democratic in as far as they were open to any ratepayer who cared to attend. There were far fewer ratepayers in proportion to the present-day population, as not many people in those days had the privilege of owning land or property.

The Manorial system was done away with in 1863 when the current system of local government came into being.

1809 - The Beginning of the Reigate Fire Brigade
The story of Reigate's Fire Brigade begins in the early 1800s. On the 8th of November, 1809, at a Vestry meeting held to make a rate for the relief of the poor, consideration was also given to, *'the necessity of appointing proper persons to work and keep in use the fire engines now deposited in the Markit (sic) House of Reigate, the aforesaid being the gift of the Right Honourable John Lord Somers and the Right Honourable Philip Earl of Hardwicke, assisted by a small subscription from the Insurance Office, for the use of the inhabitants of the parish of Reigate against any fire that might happen within the said Parish.'*

It is interesting to note that the meeting was at the Rose and Crown, an inn at 42-44 High Street, Reigate, dating from around 1700, and disappearing around 1900. There is no information about whether the presentation of these machines was expected but it must be assumed that some event, probably the loss of the cage and its water supply, had prompted their Lordships to make such a donation.

Parish officials present at this meeting were the Churchwarden, Thomas Paley; the Guardian, James Knowles, and two overseers, Richard Drewett and Henry Holdsworth. Also present were local inhabitants James Relf, James Turner, Thomas Neale, Richard Dewdney, William Beale, Joseph Coulstock and Abel Garraway.

Their resolution was, *'that the churchwardens for the time being shall see that the engines shall be kept in good order and fitting for use at the time it may happen they might be wanted, and that the following persons are hereby appointed to work and keep the said engines in use, viz: Charles Briggs, Thomas Heather, George Holdsworth, James Butwell, William Allwork, John Holding.*

If the list of persons present were complete then it would seem that these men were named in their absence. If they were willing appointees then it is assumed they had indicated that willingness prior to the meeting. Some, at least, were probably public minded men, for William Allwork was an Overseer in 1818 and, in 1823, appointed a Guardian of the Poor. In a history of the Reigate Fire Brigade written by Fred Legg in the 1930s, when he was a serving officer, he states that these names were still to be found in the town as being borne by the descendants of these original fire fighters.

At the same meeting it was also resolved *'that when the above persons are called out they shall receive five shillings each person for each time as the said engines are wanted in order to keep them in use as aforesaid'.*

As a result of this meeting the town's first fully official, organised and paid fire fighting force had been brought into being. But the money to pay the men had to be found, and so, in that same year of 1809, there was a further resolution, *'that notice be given in the church on Sunday the 19th instant for a vestry of the Town and Foreign after Divine Service in the morning to consider the proper means to defray the expense of paying the aforesaid persons.'*

This subsequent meeting had present only three persons who were at the meeting of the 8th; the Guardian, James Knowles, Churchwarden Thomas Paley, and local inhabitant William Beale. They represented the Borough of Reigate along with one Richard Thornton. Representing the Foreign was Churchwarden Joseph Nash, Overseer Thomas Wright and three others, Thomas Knight, Robert Fuller and James Symonds. Together they resolved, *'that the fire engines be worked about two or three times in each year and that the parties appointed to work and keep in use the same shall be paid 5/- each man for each time the said engines shall be worked and used in the manner aforesaid'.* It was also resolved *'that all expenses attending the said engines and the keeping in use the same to be paid by the Borough and Foreign in equal proportions.'*

The above resolutions are a little lacking in wording specific enough to be sure that the men were being paid 5/- each time they were working the engines *to keep them in use,* and 5/- each time they called to use them to fight a fire. Also, the case for whether this last resolution about the sharing of the costs was fair or not is a little uncertain. The local population was mainly centred in the Old Borough, which comprised the 400 acres of Reigate Town. As the fire engines were both kept in the Old Borough it must have required relatively little time to deal with a fire there when compared with the travelling time to the sparsely populated 6000 acres of the Foreign. And because the population was so much denser in the Old Borough it might be assumed that the majority of the fires would be there. It might appear, therefore, that the Old Borough was getting its fire needs subsidised by the Foreign.

As far as the men working the engines were concerned, if given the choice, a fire in Reigate town must have been much preferred to a fire in the Foreign as their payment for each occasion was fixed and the town option entailed much less travelling. Also, unlike at the previous meeting, these appointees were not named, so it is not known if they were to be different men or the same ones. It would make sense at least for them to be the same ones who would man the engines to fight fires in order that they might become that much more familiar with the machines, but again no reference is made to this point in the resolution.

With regard to the question of how regular the testing was, bearing in mind that fires might occur between tests, it has been noted from the records of other towns that routine tests were carried out at the specified intervals regardless of actual use at fires. This, probably, was an interpretation of the rules that ensured that the money to be paid was indeed earned.

Further information about these fire engines cannot be obtained from the records of future Vestry meetings for the Parish of Reigate, as although such records exist from 1790 through to 1920 the references discussed on these pages are the only ones appearing in them. This is explained by the fact that under Acts of the 1830s the old Manorial Inspectors of Lighting were authorised to levy taxes for the purpose of paying for local services. Although there was no specific reference in the Acts to fire prevention it seems that fairly early on the Vestry was relieved of responsibility for bearing the costs incurred by the engines by this other body. The inspectors of lighting soon became part of the Watch Committee, which also kept records, but those records survive only for the years 1864 to 1913 and 1939 to 1941 when the brigade was nationalised and became the responsibility of the Secretary of State. As far as the period from 1809 to 1864 is concerned the only source of information remains the Churchwardens Accounts.

Nevertheless it was, in 1809 as previously stated, that the Churchwardens were charged with seeing *'that the fire engines be worked about two or three times in each year'*, and given the responsibility of paying for this duty. As genuine use of the fire engines was not to be predicted it is assumed that 'working the engines' was intended as a routine procedure to keep them in good order. This routine was referred to as *'practising the engines'* in the first reference to it in the Churchwarden's records for 1809. There were two payments made for 'practising', one of 10/6d and another of £2-15-0.

The word 'practising' gave way to other words eventually. 'Working' the engines was used, as was 'attending' to them. Although payments were made *for* every year, they were not always made regularly. In 1858, for example, payment had not been made for four years, and the complete sum due from the Old Borough - one half of the total, the cost being shared with the Foreign - was paid in one lump. Churchwardens records for the Foreign have not survived, so they cannot be used to supply extra information.

The men carrying out the year-to-year maintenance of the engines are occasionally named. Of those originally nominated for the task - Charles Briggs, Thomas Heather, George Holdsworth, James Butwell, William Allwork, and John Holding - it is the third of those, George Holdsworth, whose name is the earliest and most common. Until 1832 he was, with others, being paid for working the engines. In 1826 Messrs Doubells and Thornton (the latter present at the second of the 1809 meetings) were the only interruption to George's reign. Charles Miller was the one of the team who was paid from 1833 to 1838, C. Briggs, H. Fuller, Richard Purcier, Bill Bryant and Richard Turner being named individually or together after that. The latter was the last to be involved in the final years of these records up to 1857.

Their payment at first was, of course, the 5/- per man per occasion originally specified in 1809.

This amounted to £2-10-0 per year for five men completing the task twice yearly. This payment remained the same at least until 1855.

Repairs were needed to the engines[5], and surprisingly they were necessary in 1809, their very first year as public machines. William Coulstock was paid 10s 4d for 'oiling the pipes', and Mr N. Coulstock was paid 9/- for 'engine sharps', whatever they were. These men were possibly sons of the Joseph Coulstock who had been present at the first of the 1809 meetings. Then, in 1810, James Turner was paid 10s 1d for 'iron for the engine shafts', presumably meaning the shafts between which the horse (or horses) would be harnessed.

These very early repairs raise conjecture that the engines were not new in 1809. If they were not then were had they come from? As Lords Somers and Hardwicke had donated them there is a possibility that those worthies had previously employed the engines on their own estates, had replaced them with newer machines and given the old ones to the people of Reigate. They could, of course, have obtained them elsewhere but certainly second-hand it would seem they were, for if work was required on them why were the necessary repairs not referred back to a recent manufacturer?

Other repairs were carried out. John Barber was paid for work in 1821, 1822 and 1823, and in 1824 Mr Hanson repaired the engine pipes. What the pipes were is not clear but Mr Hanson also received payment for bell ropes, so perhaps there's a clue there. He was paid again for the same task the following year, on the other engine presumably, unless his first job was less than satisfactory. In 1824 at least one of the engines was painted, and a Mrs Knowles was paid 15s 6d for work on the engines (not curtains, surely!)

Richard Turner, already mentioned as working the engines as late as 1857 (unless he had a son of the same name) presented two repair bills in 1828. Another previously named man, one George Holdsworth, made repairs in 1830 as well as working the engines that year. He was a carpenter by trade and as the engine construction was mainly of wood his attentions are not surprising. He again made repairs in 1836 and 1850.

Men working on the engines did other work for the public authorities. In 1833 Charles Miller received his 10/- a year for helping work the engines and also received £4 per year for keeping in repair and winding the town clock. Richard Purcier, in 1845, and William Fuller, in 1850, were paid for working and cleaning the engines and also for cleaning the local cage or prison, and for putting down clean straw for prisoners at quarter session times.

One aspect of the early days of the men of the Reigate Fire Force is their official titles. No evidence of them being paid to actually fight fires has been unearthed but they must surely have done this and therefore been entitled to be called firemen. Strangely the engines are not referred to as *fire* engines until 1814, and stranger still the word firemen is not applied in the Churchwardens' records until 1832. There is one instance in 1823 when the men working the engines are referred to as 'engineers' but is the only time the word was applied from 1809 to 1857. The Churchwardens' records were kept by people fairly closely acquainted with the men in question, so perhaps the names really were not frequently used at all.

This brings us to the fire force in general. Was it a fire brigade as such? Certainly it was in one definition of the word, which is an organised body of workers. But was there a chain of command or uniforms? Was the word 'brigade' officially used? Such questions also bring us to a new situation, apparent maybe for the first time in 1853, definitely in 1855. The Churchwardens were in office for three-year terms, and Charles Goldsmith, a name not apparent before this date, was Churchwarden from 1853 to 1855. In his first year he makes an entry:

'Fuller Wm. Fire Brigade. £2-10-0'.

Here is the very first reference to a 'Fire Brigade', accompanied by payment of the normal amount

for those years. Regarding payments for the engine, the situation is compounded by an 1855 entry:
> *'Chas Goldsmith, rent of fire engines and wine.*   £9-7-9   £8-1-8

Wine was supplied throughout the years by different people to the church for use in religious sacraments, so one of those prices can be discounted, although which is not certain. The other price is for rent of the engines and is being paid to Chas Goldsmith by the Churchwardens. Reading on to 1858 there is another, similar, entry:
> *Rent of Fire Engines, Mr Goldsmith*   *one third*   *£1-13-4*

This amount does not relate to either of the previous amounts, i.e. is not a fraction of either of them, but is still rent being paid to the same man. The records end in this year so no more checks or comparisons can be made. The 'one third' refrence might mean that only that proportion was due from the Old Borough, and that the other two thirds, i.e. £3-6-8, was due from elsewhere, presumably the Foreign.

1818-1846 - The Rise of Redhill
In 1854 there was a suggestion of the re-deployment of one of the two Reigate engines to the Foreign. Before the 1840s there was very little habitation in the Foreign, but the reason for the decision to re-define the areas of use of the engines is explained by the changes that had been taking place two miles to the east of Reigate.

In 1800 there was no Redhill and the only roads in the area skirted the low-laying swampy area where it now is. The east-west route used Mill Street, the present Hooley Lane and Redstone Hollow to reach Nutfield and points beyond, whilst the main north-south route was down Reigate Hill, through the town to Woodhatch, Sidlow and points south. There was another way north, and that lay through Reigate, on to Linkfield Corner, along Linkfield Lane and into Frenches Road, up School Hill, through Merstham High Street (Quality Street now) and along an old road to Coulsdon. In 1808 a new road was made from Coulsdon to Gatton Point, where it turned towards Reigate, joining Church Street at the bottom of Grammar School Hill.

In 1818 another new road, the present A23, was built southwards from Gatton Point to join the old Brighton-Reigate-London Road (the present A217) at Povey Cross. This road had had plenty of impact for through coaching traffic but little immediate effect on the area.

Twenty-three years later, in 1841, the London, Brighton and South Coast Railway Company (LB&SCR) built the London to Brighton railway. The following year a rail junction was formed by the addition of the South Eastern Railway Company's (SER) line to Dover. These lines originally had their own separate stations but the companies combined them at the site of the present Redhill station around 1844/5. The Railway Hotel was built alongside the new station by Richard Laker and a new access road was provided by the railway company from the old east-west road at the top of Redstone Hill down to their station and extended as far as the 1818 Gatton Point to Povey Cross road. This station access road was then further extended westwards from this junction as far as Linkfield Corner to provide better access from Reigate, and a cross-roads was therefore formed close to the station. By 1846 the nearby habitation around Linkfield Lane was being extended by the granting by Lord Monson's widow of 99 year leases on parcels of land between Linkfield Lane and North Street and the new road to Linkfield Corner (now Station Road West). The new settlement of Warwick Town arose and new roads, such as Warwick Road, were built off it.

Soon this west side development was to reach the cross-roads and, as the wet land on the eastern side of the through road was drained, extended towards the station beyond. The name Red Hill had since Saxon times been associated with the rising common land to the south, and began to be used as the alternative name for the new development. Red Hill, later to be simply Redhill, had been born.

1854 - An Engine For The Foreign?

So, back to the suggestion of an engine for the Foreign, which in reality meant the new town of Redhill. In the 1930 history of the Reigate Fire Brigade Fred Legg states that in 1854 there was a review of the then current precautions, and the Vestry decided that the services of the fire engines would be better employed if one were to be kept in the Old Borough while the other were kept in the Foreign. Six more men were to be trained so that there was a separate team for each engine, thereby doubling the size of the fire fighting force in the Borough to twelve.

In reference to the above use of the term 'fire fighting force' it ought to be pointed out here that six men could not turn up at a fire and do everything that was necessary to quench a reasonably sized blaze. The assistance of local people would have been required in the handling of the horses and machine, and massive assistance needed with the prolonged pumping of the machine and the fetching and carrying of water where not immediately available. The conception of a ''Brigade' turning up and doing all that was required to quench anything from a small, confined fire to a large conflagration while bystanders stood and watched is a modern one which must not be applied to the situation existing in earlier times.

Looking back it seems that a long time had elapsed since 1809 when two engines had been presented, and it is wondered how six men could have utilised them both. As far as this 1854 transfer is concerned, there is no direct evidence that it ever actually happened but the Churchwarden's entries for 1855 and 58 indicate that something had happened, for new arrangements were in hand. If Charles Goldsmith was being paid for rent of fire engines (note the plural) does that mean he now owned them both? And how did he acquire them? Why is there no record of payment to the Churchwardens for their purchase? And if he did not own them, what was going on?

Another factor is that the proportion of rent being paid by the Old Borough was now one third instead of one half. Had a third party taken control of one of the engines, the Vestry for the Foreign, for example, or one of the petty boroughs? If so then the Old Borough was paying one third for one engine, the Foreign was paying one third for the same engine, yet it now had an engine of its own.

The answer was that a new engine had been supplied by Shand Mason and Co. There is no way of telling this from the records of the time, all details of the transaction, and of local decisions and financial arrangements have been either lost or hidden in archives so well that they failed to surface during research. Evidence of the purchase does not appear in records until 1899 when the machine is due for extensive repairs and its history is revealed (see later in this history). Now there were three engines, two from the 1809 gifts plus this 1857 replacement.

Manual Engines

These engines were manually operated. They were water reservoirs fitted with pumps that were operated by hand; i.e. they were water transference devices and pressure generators. Water was pumped from the reservoir onto the fire. Replacement of that water could be pumped on board via a hose placed into a local pond, stream or water main, and if neither was near enough then they had to be kept topped up by bucket chain. Each machine had a pair of single acting force pumps worked by four, six or eight men exerting their efforts on long pole handles on either side of the machine. It was not easy work, especially over a long period, and at a large fire many changes of pump teams would be required. Although the machines would have been capable of being wheeled into immediate position by a number of men they would have to have been drawn to the site of the fire by two or four horses, which first would have had to have been fetched from a nearby stable.

During research into this history a number of statements have been found claiming that when fully operational a good machine could throw a 5/8 inch jet of water to a height of around 100 feet. Later in this history it is stated that even this was exceeded. Experts on this matter say differently however, pointing out that manufacturer's claims were often wildly exaggerated. Two sources may be quoted to support lesser achievements - firstly that the pressure used when testing Metropolitan Brigade manuals was 30lbs per square inch. At that pressure, when using a 5/8 inch nozzle the height of a jet can be calculated hydraulically, and tables from around 1900 show that 40 feet would be a more accurate assessment. Secondly, practical experience can be quoted, as a Newsham engine which was restored to full working order, fitted with new pistons and leathers, along with new clack valves, was hard pressed to achieve 40 feet in height.[6]

At least one of the Reigate manuals had iron bound solid disc wheels. It could have been a Newsham, a type of pump that was sometimes adapted so that one horse could pull it within attachable shafts. Its wheels were small, however, and did not allow it to be pulled very far over rough roads. It was more usual when a distance was involved to put such an engine up onto a cart with bigger wheels that could then be pulled by two or more horses. The larger wheels would better traverse rough ground and not so easily get bogged down on wintry roads that were often a muddy morass.

When two manual pumps were found in a Reigate Council yard, having been moved there from the caves off Reigate tunnel where they had been stored for many years, there was with them a large farm cart which was thought to have some connection with the engines. The farm cart is now on display at Agricultural Museum at the Reeds, just outside Farnham. Such large carts often had hinged ramps fitted with a winch used to pull the manual engine up into the cart but there was no evidence of this on the Reigate cart, so it may not have had such an association with either of the engines. More information is given about the finding of the old engines and what was done with them in a later chapter.

1857 - Getting to the Fire

Before dealing in more detail with the 1860s it is interesting to note some 1857/58 entries in a record book kept by Robert Legg, who was then Captain (or foreman) of the Reigate Brigade. These entries refer to expenses incurred in getting the engine to the fire. One item, *'Gates and candles'*, would refer to the tolls paid at the gates of the turnpike roads, for not even an engine on the way to a fire was exempt, and to the candles carried to light the way. *'Post-boys'*, or simply *'lads'*, would refer to the use of riders on additional horses when four instead of two animals were used to pull the engines because of the state of the roads. The Reigate brigade did not restrict its services to the Reigate area alone, as these expenses were incurred on journeys to fires at Dorking and Horley as well. When attending fires in districts such as Dorking or Horley, which both had their own engines, the Reigate men would have been assisting that other body.

Whereas men could ride on some engines (and can you imagine the harshness of the ride on an appliance with no suspension) the Newsham type of engine had no provision for anyone to ride on it. As previously stated it was frequently carried on a cart, which in the 19th century did have axles with leaf springs, although it would not have been over-effective in providing a smooth ride. The crews no doubt earned a fair proportion of their five shillings per call during the journey alone.

1862 - Worn Out Equipment

At least two engines remained in service but by 1862 had become less than fully efficient. This is illustrated in Fred Legg's 1930s history by the events of 30th November 1861, when the Reigate brigade was called to a fire at Timberham House, Charlwood. After the inevitable delay incurred as the men assembled and the horses were brought up, the two engines set out. A mile and a half outside the town one engine shed a wheel. The men from that engine mounted the other and the journey continued with one engine.

Tho. Cooke Engine-Maker in ye Minories.

THOMAS COOKE, *of the Minories, London,* ENGINE-MAKER,

HAS Contrived constant Stream Engines of different Sizes, for extinguishing FIRES, both in Ships, and Houses; for Wetting Sails, Watering Gardens, or any other Use to which Engines may be applied, the Mechanism of which, is of such a Nature, as not easily to be put out of Order, and consequently quickly rectified; the Largest of Which, may be drawn thro' a Passage of Three Feet wide, in Compleat Working Order, and the small Sorts in Proportion.

The SIZES and PRICES are as follow,

Sizes.	Men to Work each	Gallons discharged in a Minute.	Distance in Yards.	Price with 6 Feet of Sucking Pipe.			Advanced Price with 40 Foot of Hose, and Brass Screws included.		
				l.	*s.*	*d.*	*l.*	*s.*	*d.*
First	4	50	23	12	00	00	2	00	00
Second	6	60	30	16	00	00	2	00	00
Third	10	65	35	26	00	00	3	06	00
Fourth	16	80	40	36	00	00	3	10	00
Fifth	20	100	50	45	00	00	4	00	00

N.B. The Addition of a Copper Fan (which may be put on, or taken off at pleasure) makes it very useful for Watering Gardens, &c.

Prices of ENGINES for Shipping, or Watering Gardens, to be worked by one or two Men.
First, the Squirt ENGINE with Twelve Feet of Forcing Hose, and Brass Screws ———— 5*l.*
Second, Constant Stream ENGINE with Twelve Feet of Hose ———— 7
Third ENGINE and 12 Feet of Hose and Fan ———— 10

Likewise Makes all Sorts of Leather Buckets, to fill the ENGINES with Water, and Leather Pipes; Also all Sorts of ENGINE Buckets, or Hose repaired at reasonable Rates.

Early hand operated fire pump
The picture used for this advertisement shows an early manual fire engine in use.

Upon arrival the work of pumping water and directing it onto the fire began but the pump broke down. With a carter, one of the firemen returned to the other engine, some eight miles back. A nail was used as a lynchpin and the engine taken back to Charlwood where the fire was extinguished - presumably not so much of a task by this time as it must have been almost burnt out after the delay.

Fred Legg goes on to say that the state of the two old engines became a matter of public concern, which is not surprising considering the foregoing story. At an 1862 meeting in the Reigate Public Hall it was decided to buy an up-to-date manual engine with money raised by public subscription. The meeting was called by, or was under the patronage of, a Mr John Lees, and the type of machine that it was decided to buy was a 'Shand Mason', a machine produced by a London company that was established in 1851 and run by a Mr Shand and a Mr Mason. There is evidence that the latter gentleman might have been a Redhill Resident.

A question is now raised about the previous 'new' engine, the one previously refered to as having been purchased in 1857. Where was it? Fred Legg's history reveals no mention of the 1857 purchase, and there is no reference in official records to it at the 1862 meeting. Is it possible that the 1854 transfer had taken place and the new engine was now in the Foreign, leaving two old engines at Reigate? This possibility would not seem to be supported by the fact that by 1866 the Redhill Brigade was in need of a new engine, and in 1868 was in receipt of one. And it is further undermined by the fact that years later, in 1899, it was a *Reigate* engine that was to be identified by Shand Mason as being supplied by them in 1857.

Whatever the fact of the 1857 engine, it remains a puzzle

Notes to Chapter One

[1] *Fire hooks with horses attached were often used to collapse buildings by attaching the hook to an iron ring fitted to the apex of the gable end of a timber-framed house. This would help to create a break against the further spread of fire. There are still a few old houses about with the iron ring still in position in other counties. Kingston, Guildford and Haslemere all have local records confirming the possession of fire hooks, but none mounted on wheels.*

[2] *It is said that Haslemere has records of a local man who had some timber 'flues' and was regularly fined at each Michaelmas sittings for still having them in position against the law.*

[3] *This was not the first patent, for that had been granted in 1625. By 1666 one maker alone had produced over sixty fire pumps. See article in 'Vigiles', the magazine of the Surrey Fire Preservation Trust, Issue 1, 1997, which contains an article on this subject.*

[4] *Contours on a 6 inch Ordnance map would show the distance in height between the Reigate Castle moat and the cage. Multiplying the height difference in feet by 0.462 would give the pressure in lb./sq" at the cage, or roughly 1lb for every 2 feet. The local cage was often the location for a small engine house and it is wondered if there was a small manual pump housed by the Reigate cage. The castle moat was used again in the Second World War as an emergency fire fighting water supply, involving the fitting of a pipeline and a sluice gate.*

[5] *It is relevant here to mention that since the 1788 beginning of this record book there had been no other mention of an 'engine', so the word being used for the first time in 1809 can only have referred to the fire engines.*

[6] *During research a letter was found stating that a repaired engine threw a jet over the tower of a Reigate church.*

Chapter Two

Into the Second Half of the 19th Century

Incorperation and its Effects

Within a few years, certainly by 1854, Warwick Town, as Redhill was first known, had grown considerably in size and population and it was clear that the new town to the east of Reigate was no false starter. It would seem reasonable to assume, therefore, that the 1854 proposal regarding the division of the fire engines' services was brought about by the increase in population in this new town. But however good this assumption may be, and however great a need it was designed to fulfil, it seems that if this transfer ever actually took place then it was later reversed. Evidence for this is that in 1864 the newly created Council was again proposing that one of the fire engines from the Old Borough should be used in the new town.

What had happened in those ten years was that the local administrative power had been mainly wrested from the grasp of the Parish and the Manor by the formation towards the end of 1863 of a Borough Council. Local people, many of them drawn to the area by the boom in land and property prices of the new-town development taking place, and by the prospect of business opportunities, were dissatisfied with the state of affairs that existed. Problems of inequality of voting and property rights, of the lack of services such as lighting, main drainage and sewerage, were the factors that had made people dissatisfied. Fuelling this dissatisfaction was the spread of education and newspapers, both of which made people more socially and politically aware. They petitioned the Government for, and obtained, a Charter of Incorporation that empowered them to set up the body of accountable Aldermen and Councillors that, Aldermen apart, still exists today. The new, democratic body replaced the old, undemocratic system of rule by the rich and privileged.

That the wealthy upper class felt bitterness and resentment over the change is not in doubt. Divisions were created that lasted many years and were manifested in a rivalry between the two towns of Reigate and Redhill as well as between the two factions who had fought over the retention of the status quo for the few or the complete change to accountability to all. Class awareness was at a pitch not known today. Even a wealthy and successful tradesman could be looked down upon because he *was* a tradesman and not one of the gentry, a group of people who considered themselves to be an elite class in whose hands, by right so they thought, all power ought to have remained.

Power had been transferred, however, and the effect was that the newly elected Reigate Borough Council was to take over many of the services previously administered by the Manor, the Fire Brigade being no exception.

1854-1866 - Fire Brigade Take-Over by the Corporation

Records of the Council meeting of the 26th June 1864 note the following: *'Upon motion by Mr Alderman Steer the question was that the late inspectors of lighting of the Old Borough be requested to deliver over to the Watch Committee one of the fire engines for the use of Warwick Town and its neighbourhood.'* This was resolved in the affirmative, i.e. a vote gaining a majority consent. Bearing in mind that there was animosity between the new and the old administrations, it might be as well to examine the wording of this request. The inspectors are referred to as *'the late inspectors'*, inferring that their status no longer existed, but they are being requested to *'deliver to the Watch Committee'*, so they had to still exist in a manner that allowed them still to have control of the fire engines, and in a way which precluded the new (less than a year old) Council from simply appropriating them.

The old Manorial Inspectors were originally involved because under Acts of the 1830s the

Inspectors of Lighting and Watching were not only empowered to make provision for the supply and upkeep of fire engines and appliances but to levy taxes for the purpose of paying for the fire service. But if the old Inspectors had not voted to relinquish their powers to the new Council then to give up the objects of their power (the fire engines) they would thereby put themselves at least partially, if not fully out of a job.

This situation was not immediately resolved for at the Council meeting of 17th October of the same year of 1864 there is another entry of very similar nature: *'Upon a motion by Councillor Boult, the late Inspectors of Lighting of the Old Borough of Reigate be requested to hand over the fire engines to the Town Council as Inspectors of Lighting for the time being.'* Again a majority consent to the motion was obtained. This is more specific, as we now see that the Council now considers itself the Inspectorate of Lighting and the old Inspectors to be defunct.

In July of the same year, following receipt of a letter by the corporation from the late Inspectors of Lighting of the Old Borough, it was resolved that *'the Local Board take to the fire engines lately under the control of the late Inspectors of Lighting acting for the Old Borough'.* If the meaning of this is not quite clear then we can refer to Fred Legg's history for clarification. It states that, on November 3rd, 1864, a notice was sent out to fire brigade members requiring them to hand over the fire engine, their uniforms and accoutrements. They refused, saying that they were not appointed by the new-fangled Corporation, nor had the existing engine been supplied by it. The result of their defiance was that they woke up one day soon after this to find that the door of the engine house had been forced and the engine put under lock and key elsewhere.

Also according to Fred Legg, the existing fire brigade was dismissed. This would have created a situation where not only was there no official fire brigade, nor would there have been one in practice because the men and their engine were separated. What would have happened if there had been a fire at this time? Would the engine have been made available to the 'rebels'? Would they have fought the fire and restored their advantage afterwards by hiding their precious engine themselves? Or would they have returned it in a rush of reconciliation and been re-instated and as the new and official brigade members?

What is also interesting to note is that the engine is referred to in the singular in the above. Bearing in mind that a new (third) engine had been bought in 1857, and it was only in the previous year that a decision to buy a another new one had been made, and only in the June of the current year that Alderman Steer had requested that one of the engines be handed over to the Watch Committee for use in Redhill Town, it is wondered what the situation really was regarding the whereabouts at this time of all of the engines.

Fred Legg's account continues by recording that the result of the November, 1864, action was that the corporation announced that it was forming a new Reigate Brigade under the captaincy of Mr J.H.Apted, and issued a notice inviting men to apply for posts. Some of the members of the previously existing brigade joined the new one, among them Edwin Legg, son of the previous captain. The new captain, Job Heath Apted, must have been a busy man, for on the 5th of February, 1864, he had been appointed Inspector of Nuisances and Collector of Highway and District Rates.

Unfortunately, research failed to find any directly corroborative evidence to confirm Fred Legg's account. This is not to say that his account is inaccurate, just that it would have been nice to see something written in the minutes of either the Watch Committee, begun in January 1864, or the minutes of the full council, which started one month earlier in December 1863.

An important point to make here is that at this time there was still just the one Borough Brigade, it was not until 1865 that the question of a separate force for each town of Redhill and

Engineer Edmund Worsfold, Redhill Brigade

Reigate arose. At a meeting of townsmen at the Tower Inn, Redhill, on 18th April of that year the decision was taken to inaugurate such a separate force, to be called 'The Redhill Volunteer Fire Brigade'. The personnel were to consist of Superintendent, Foreman, Engineer, Sub-Engineer and at least eight firemen. This raises the immediate question: - would a brigade have been constituted without an engine? The answer might seem unlikely to be 'yes' but in the Watch Committee minutes of the 24th April, 1865, is the entry: *'Resolved that the Mayor be requested to ascertain who has custody of the fire engines and whether they cannot be placed under the control of the Council'*.

It must be remembered that at this stage, six full months after the formation of the Council, not all organisation was in concert, and the creation of a Redhill Brigade was probably done outside of the Council's jurisdiction, that body and the people having yet to fully integrate their efforts and intent. The actual possession of an engine by Redhill in 1865, on the other hand, whether within or without the circle of the Council's control, could well have given rise to exactly the same requirement to form a force to man it as had been the case in Reigate in 1809. This, then, seems to be the evidence, albeit indirect, that is required to corroborate Fred Legg's account of slightly earlier events. [1]

Just as the proposal to form a Redhill Brigade was made in 1865 it is also feasible that the formation of a Redhill Brigade could have been proposed years before in 1854, when it had been proposed to keep one engine in the Old Borough (Reigate) and the other in the Foreign (Redhill). The fact that it was not formed would equally suggest that no such transfer took place.

Evidence that an engine was at Redhill five months later can be read in the records of the time. There had to be a permanent home for the new town's fire engine, and in a motion proposed by Cllr Young at a Council meeting of 9th September, 1865, it was proposed *'that the Watch Committee be empowered to carry into effect their recommendation as to a watch house and lock-up cells at Warwick Town to include a shed for the fire engines and water carts at a cost not to exceed £400'*.

One of the first tasks the new Council had set itself was to form its own police force but a proper police station in the town had not yet been provided. When the watch-house and cells were built the opportunity was taken to house the fire engine at the same time. A contract was awarded to one Thomas Penfold for the erection of the police accommodation and presumably an engine shed. The job was finished in May, 1865 and £200, possibly a second part-payment, was paid to Mr Penfold for this work in February of 1866.

Returning to the matter of the loyalty of the members of the Fire Brigades of both towns; in February of 1866 it is reported in Watch Committee minutes that the leaders of the two Brigades were to be present at its next meeting. This they duly were, and on 24th May 1866, the representative of the Reigate Brigade stated that his colleagues in that town were willing to serve under the Council. The Redhill Brigade representative were not quite as positive, saying only that he thought members probably were willing. This is slightly surprising when it is considered that previous resistance had come from the Reigate men, but seems to have been good enough for the subsequent resolution: *'to accept the engines, three in number, of the late inspectors, and to continue the services of the existing Fire Brigades until further notice, they having consented to do so.'*

And magically there are three engines once more.

Fortunately for us the minutes also contained the names of the members of both forces.

It was recorded that the Reigate Brigade consisted of: -

Mr Job Heath Apted	*Rank not mentioned, but in charge.*
Mr Cheal	*Position uncertain but possibly secretary of the Reigate Brigade, perhaps having previously been a lighting inspector under the old manorial system.*
Frederick Fuller	*Foreman*
Richard Turner Jnr	*Sub Engineer*
George Tichener	*No shown position but assumed to have been a fireman.*
William Peters	*No shown position but assumed to have been a fireman.*
James Brooker	*No shown position but assumed to have been a fireman.*
George Joyes	*Reserve*
William Monk	*Reserve*
George Thrift	*Reserve*

The Redhill Brigade was comprised of: -

Mr Levi Collins	*Superintendent*
Josias Markwick	*Secretary of the Reigate Brigade, perhaps also having previously been a lighting inspector under the old manorial system.*
William Fuller	*Foreman*
Mr Wilkinson	*Engineer*
Mr Elmslie	*Sub-engineer*
Mr Mulley	*No shown position but assumed to have been a fireman.*
Mr Edward Lambert	*No shown position but assumed to have been a fireman.*
Mr Topliss	*No shown position but assumed to have been a fireman.*
Richard Bailey	*No shown position but assumed to have been a fireman.*
Mr I. G. Sanders	*No shown position but assumed to have been a fireman.*
F. Coluom (sic)	*No shown position but assumed to have been a fireman.*
Mr Robins	*No shown position but assumed to have been a fireman.*

Whatever the uncertainties of the past there was now agreement and stability as far as the personnel of the Fire Brigades of the two towns of the Borough of Reigate were concerned.

1866-67 - Fire Engines Still Worn Out

Unfortunately the situation was not so settled where the equipment was concerned, for on the 22nd of August 1866, a letter was written to the corporation about a fire in Linkfield Lane. The letter was written on behalf of the Fire Brigade by Josias Markwick who, from the list above we see was closely connected with the Redhill force. He was also a Redhill High Street grocer who had also recently been appointed as deputy to Thomas Weller, the Reigate Borough Assessor of Rates. Part of the letter drew attention to the fact that there was insurance money to be collected, but it also laid out the shortcomings of the ancient fire engine. The letter was referred to the Watch Committee meeting of 29th of August, to which Messrs Markwick and Wilkinson went as a deputation to verbally express concern over the defective condition and insufficient power of the Redhill engine.

Which of the three engines had Redhill received from Reigate? It would seem not to be the 1857 purchase, and surely not the defective engine replaced by that purchase. That leaves one other engine that we know dated from at least 1809 and may not have been new then, so it is of little surprise that it was not up to scratch.

The Watch Committee reported to the Corporation at the 19th November full council meeting that they recommended the purchase of a replacement machine, but Councillor Austen had other ideas. He proposed that the purchase not be approved. His reason was that mains water was soon to be laid to Redhill; plans for this were already in hand and, he argued, it would be foolish to spend money on a new engine when water at a reasonable pressure for fighting fires would soon be readily available. His proposition received enough support to be carried.

So by April 1867 a new engine had still not been bought. The Watch Committee noted in their minutes that they were awaiting the Council's instructions on the matter, and were in the meantime deputising Councillors Steers and Trower to point out the spots in the town where the first fireplugs, forerunners of today's hydrants, were to be placed. This those worthies did, making nineteen recommendations. Alderman Baker then proposed that as an alternative to the purchase of a new engine Mr Shand be asked to examine the old one as to the possibility of repairs and advise the Watch Committee accordingly.

The previously mentioned 1862 meeting at Reigate had resolved to replace an old engine and had said that a Shand-Mason engine should be bought. It seems more than likely that the engine Mr Shand was asked to examine was very possibly the very same engine. He was no doubt from Shand-Mason, the fire engine manufacturers, and it seems highly unlikely that he would be disposed to do his own firm out of profits by recommending repair work rather than the purchase of a new machine. It comes as no surprise, therefore, that his recommendation, when given to the first council meeting of 1867, was that a new machine should be bought and the old one repaired.

Once again Councillor Austen was having none of this and proposed 'that it is not expedient to proceed with the purchase of a new engine and appliances at present'. The meeting was still with him, for once again his motion was carried.

Six months later, however, the situation had changed. Councillor Thornton proposed that an efficient fire engine be procured for use of the Corporation, to be stationed in the eastern ward (Redhill). His reasoning could well have been that in spite of water being laid to the town there were still plenty of places on its edges, and in what was still a very rural area beyond, where the nearest well, stream or pond was still the only water source, the need for a pump therefore still being required. Councillor Austen, true to form, still opposed such a move but this time was defeated. A new engine was to be bought. In November 1866 it was resolved that notices were to be placed in *The Engineer* and *The Times* inviting tenders for a new engine.

Merryweather horse drawn manual advertisement

Another event of this time was an application from a Mr Nisei of Salford Mill to buy the number three engine. It was considered advisable that the engine should be sold and a Mr Batchelor was authorised to negotiate the sale. Records of that year are silent on the matter of his success but records of 1869 show <u>two</u> old engines for sale, so it seems safe to assume that the original sale did not proceed.

Also at this time Mr Apted, the Reigate Superintendent, previously the Captain of the Reigate Brigade when it was the only Brigade, and who in the Watch Committee minutes was curiously referred to as the *Inspector* of the Reigate Brigade (the only time this title appears) [2] tendered his resignation, reason unrecorded. He was asked to remain in office until a replacement was found.

The advertisement in *The Engineer* and *The Times* seem not to have had satisfactory results for in August 1867 further adverts were placed in *Builder, Engineer* and two local newspapers, again inviting tenders for a new engine. This did the trick for in February of 1868 the new machine had arrived. [3] The manufacturer of the new engine is uncertain because it seems to have been supplied via the local firm of Marriage and Wood.[4]

With a new engine and a new shed in which to keep it, Redhill's Fire Brigade was well and truly born. Unfortunately the suitability of the engine shed was in question, with the engine difficult to get out and harness horses to because of the narrowness of the access way. This had been recognised in January, before the engine arrived, probably when the shed was ready for occupation and an attempt had been made to put the old engine in it. A sub-committee of the Mayor, Alderman Lambert, with Councillors Austen and Steer was deputed to find a suitable place for the fire engine. The chosen location was Mr Topliss' coach house in West Street, Redhill. Mr Topliss ran the George and Dragon (now the Dragon) pub in West Street, which was later renamed Cromwell Road, so the coach house was presumably nearby.

The problem of a suitable fire station for Redhill would be a continuing one. Shortly after the turn of the century there were concerted efforts being made to alleviate the situation with the purchase of suitable land within the town centre upon which to build a combined police and fire station. These efforts were to be prolonged and did not result in a new building being opened in London Road until as late as 1932, sixty-odd years later. Details of the efforts to find a suitable new site are contained in a later chapter.

In 1867 investment in the Fire Brigade continued. A sub-committee was set up to look into the outfit of the men and £10 per annum was designated as payment for cleaning and oiling the fire engines, attending to hose and hydrants and generally keeping things in good order. This might not sound a great deal by today's standards but was the equivalent of around £2,000 a year. Apart from this allowance wages were also paid, although to whom is not clear. The amount was in stark contrast to the previous one, as the bill for 1st year's pay to each brigade was a mere £12, most of the firemen being volunteers working for Queen and country.

The setting up of the brigades was good for local business. William Vosper of Redhill tendered for various articles of clothing, including hats and helmets, while Lashmar's and Alfred Breach, also of Redhill, tendered for boots. Reigate firms tendered likewise. Oil, grease and candles were supplied from the towns, so much of the money spent by the Council stayed local.

The two old engines that were put up for sale in 1869 became the responsibility of Messrs Elmslie and Batchelor, who were deputed to negotiate their disposal. One was sold to the Philanthropic School the following year for £20. It must have continued to give reasonable service because thirty-nine years later, in 1909, school members were to turn up with it at a fire at Trower's warehouse in Earlswood to assist the local fire brigade. The other engine remained unsold. An 1873 motion before the Watch Committee to procure pressure nozzles for '*the two engines*' indicated only that two engines were considered as workers, and in 1874 the unsold engine was again put up for sale, this time by auction, an action that was suspended later in the year.

What actually happened to the engine is unknown, but it is noted that in February 1875 £5.50 was received for the hire of a fire engine. There had been a number of occasions when there had been requests for the hire of engines to be used as attractions at carnivals and suchlike events, most of which had been refused. It may have been that it had occurred to the council that with a lick of paint an old engine might suddenly become a source of income. As half a year's pay for one brigade was £6, and the annual rent for the standing room of the Redhill engine was also £6, one set of hire fees almost paid for one of these items of expenditure. The fact that the remaining old engine was retained for this purpose is pure speculation, however, and no corroboration of this idea has been found. If it was not the case then the details of the going of that old engine are unknown.

Divisions in the New Borough

Having mentioned wards, a short explanation is appropriate. Under the 1863 Charter of Incorporation two electoral wards were set up, an east ward and a west ward. The dividing line passed through a point on the Croydon Road at its junction with Wray Lane and continued in a manner which corresponded roughly to the areas of Reigate in the west and Redhill in the east. These would later become the areas for the individual brigades of the Borough of Reigate defining them as 'Divisions'. 'A' Division was Reigate while 'B' Division was Redhill.

The term 'The Borough of Reigate' now referred to the new corporation which administered the affairs of two towns and surrounding lands, not just one town and the Foreign as before. Perhaps this is a good point to refer to the then Lords of the Manor, Lord Somers, who owned great areas of Reigate, and Lord Monson, or his successors, who owned similar tracts in Redhill. Their holdings remained, of course, as did their wealth; it was their power and influence that was curtailed. They had fought against incorporation because of their vested interests but had lost. Their power was now in the hands of that collective body of Councillors and Aldermen already mentioned who formed the Reigate Borough Corporation, and the destiny of those men was in the hands of the electorate. This Council was now, and presumably still is, effectively the Lord of the Manor, although that was a title that increasingly fell from use and from memory.

1867 - Town Water Supplies and the Predecessor of the Hydrant.

Water had been provided in the Old Borough for a number of years by the Reigate Water Company, but its supplies had never extended beyond Reigate. The new corporation had resolved that water should be provided to the Foreign - which effectively meant Redhill, then still known as Warwick Town - and this was done by the Caterham Spring Water Company in 1867. At a Watch Committee meeting on the 23rd of April, 1867, prior to the laying of the water mains, Alderman Howard proposed that 'application be made to the Caterham Spring Water Company to place fire plugs at every one hundred yards in every street in Warwick Town where their mains are to be laid'. Once again it was a matter that was referred to the Watch Committee, the outcome being that it was instructed in July to do whatever was necessary to get the fire plugs in place.

1867-1875 - Job Heath Apted

As already stated, the new Reigate Brigade was formed in November, 1864, under the Captaincy or Superintendency of Mr J.H.Apted. It was also noted that he was a busy man and perhaps pressure of work was the reason for him tendering his resignation in April, 1867, as *Inspector* of the Western Ward Fire Brigade. The term 'Inspector' is only recorded this once and is assumed to either be a

Early photograph of the Borough Brigade

reversion to terms previously used in the old manorial days when the Inspectors of Lighting were responsible for the fire engines, or a confusion with his other responsibility as Inspector of Nuisances and Collector of Highway and District Rates. Another possibility is that there was some connection with the old Inspectors of Lighting that still existed and which he technically held, and that this resignation removed an anomaly. This is made uncertain by the fact that the records also note that he was asked to continue until a replacement could be found. If the Inspector rank he held was indeed archaic, it might have been that the Council was only too keen to drop it at the first opportunity. Nothing seems to have actually happened regarding his resignation because he remained in post until March 1870, when he again tendered his resignation, this time as Superintendent of Reigate Fire Brigade, only to verbally withdraw it in April and be officially re-instated in May, two months later.

Then he resigned again on 10th February 1872. The Watch Committee responded by appointing William H. Apted, presumably a relative, to the post. This was all very well except that he does not seem to have taken it up because Job heath Apted continued sending in letters in his capacity of Superintendent of the Reigate Brigade. Five more years were to pass before November 1875 when there was another letter from Mr Apted suggesting that Mr Charles Roper Mead of the Market Place, Reigate, be appointed the next Superintendent of the Western Ward (Reigate) Fire Brigade. This, finally, was the last of Mr Apted in the post but not the start of Mr Mead, as in the following March Mr Frederick Fuller was promoted from foreman to fill the post.

1875 was a time of considerable change, for at the same time the top man in the Eastern Ward of Redhill was also re-appointed, with Mr William Vosper, the Redhill trader who had been a tenderer for clothing to the Fire Brigade, becoming the new Superintendent there. What had happened to Mr Levi Collins is unknown.

1875-1886 - Day-to-Day Activities

The business of the two Brigades continued through the late 1870s and into the 1880s, most of that business being the ordinary activities necessary to maintain the force. Letters were submitted regarding fire escapes, new rules were drawn up and printed, contractors were paid for ongoing engine repairs and new ladders purchased to make the Redhill Brigade equal in equipment to Reigate. Water in the two towns was supplied by different companies using different connections, so standpipes were adapted and supplied to both engines so that either could be connected to the pipes of both towns. New helmets were procured for the Eastern Ward Brigade and new suits purchased for both. Neither fire engine was fitted with brakes and in 1884 tenders for their provision were sought. Local firm Burtenshaw and Sons offered to fit a brake and remove it at no cost if it proved unsatisfactory. Perhaps this offer applied only to the Reigate machine, for in 1888 more tenders were being submitted for a brake for the Redhill engine.

These were times when, just like today, not all members of the public were as well behaved as they might have been. The Town Clerk was asked to look into what powers existed to restrain the dangerous use of bicycle velocipedes, and the Chief Constable was asked to take steps to render the High Street more orderly on a Saturday night.

In February of 1881 William Vosper, now Captain of the Redhill Brigade but still in the tailoring business, was again supplying the Brigade with clothing. He apparently did it with not quite the alacrity of previous years as in November the Town Clerk was writing to him stating a date on which it had to be delivered.

The name of William Vosper crops up once more in 1885 when he resigns as *Superintendent* of the Redhill Brigade. In all cases the rank of an officer has been written in this history as it was written in the various records consulted but in this year of 1885 there seems to have been both a

Redhill's horse drawn manual outside the Market Hall Redhill. Note the boy peering between the legs of the rearmost fireman.

Superintendent and a Captain in the Redhill Brigade. Perhaps this had always been the case, hence the confusion over the matter. What happened upon the resignation of William Vosper was that he was asked to remain in post until a successor was found. In July 1885, when Mr H.R.Charlwood became the new Superintendent of Redhill he was asked at once to nominate a Captain of the same Brigade. At the next meeting of the Watch Committee a Mr Thomas Saunders was announced as the said Captain. Mr Vosper was asked to hand over all appliances and other articles under his control to the new Superintendent but apparently showed the same lack of alacrity in the matter as he had with the clothing of four years before, and had to be written to by the Town Clerk in the October to comply with this request.

There is a possibility that there is more to these incidents than meets the eye, and were they apparent the story would be more greatly unfolded. Until such time as the more information is uncovered the amount of information will remain meagre. As far as the situation of a Superintendent *and* a Captain at Redhill is concerned, it is noted that back at the 1864 meeting, when the members of the Brigades stated that they were prepared to work under the new Council, both Brigades had two men mentioned before the rank of Foreman on the respective lists. Although the Reigate man was listed as Secretary, it is wondered why the two ranks were necessary. One theory is that the Superintendent was less of a working fireman and more of a link between his Brigade and the Watch Committee, whereas the Captain was more of a working fireman who also acted as an technical interface between the Brigade and the Superintendent.

In 1885 cards were printed with the names and addresses of the members of the Fire Brigade, to be displayed at fire stations and elsewhere. The following January was, perhaps, a particularly cold one as there was a decision made to look into the possibility of heating the Reigate engine house. One year later the foreman of the Redhill Brigade was being asked to resign, reasons unspecified.

1809-1902 - The Engine Shed At Reigate
Reigate's station was apparently also unsatisfactory, for in the May of 1887 surveyors were asked to provide designs for a new fire station there. Plans had been in hand for some time, for it was in November 1873 when the Watch Committee appointed the Mayor, Frederick Besley, and two others - Mr Whately and Mr C. Gifford - to look into the possibility of providing a station for the Reigate engine. Presumably a more satisfactory and permanent site was required as the present standing room for the engine was rented from a Mr William Howell at £12 per year payable six- monthly. The 1874 Kelly's Directory for Surrey and Sussex shows the old station's address for that year as the Square, Reigate, which would have been the Market Place in the centre of the town. This could refer to a site at or very close to the White Hart Hotel, it being that establishment which supplied horses to the Reigate Brigade for many years. An Allingham Directory of the 1880s places the new fire station on the south side of the High Street between the Congregational Church and the police station. A more precise date for the move would be 1886/7, as in July 1887 tenders were invited for the provision of iron gates for the new Reigate fire station. The firm of Thomas Dann Heathfield won the tender at a price of £67.10s. By contrast a similar tender for gates for Redhill station was accepted from Lanaway and Sons for £7.10s. This comparison might make one suppose that the Reigate station was a much grander affair than its Redhill counterpart until the amounts the two stations were insured for are considered. Reigate's fire engine house was valued at £50 whereas Redhill's was double the amount at £100. The engines, too, had different values in favour of Redhill, although this time not so great at £200 for Reigate and £250 for Redhill. Other equipment was valued at £100 in each case, so the gate costs probably only reflect the width of frontage onto the respective roads.

Redhill crew with Captain Mason (third from right, front row) in charge

Gates aside, if Reigate could be referred to as the poor relation at this time the situation would be rectified, for fifteen years later the new Reigate fire station would open as a part of the brand new Municipal Buildings, and would become the headquarters of the Borough Brigade.

Fire Insurance and Private Fire Brigades

At this point it ought to be briefly mentioned that there were other fire fighting forces than the one whose history is dealt with here. These were fire brigades operated by or for insurance companies. After the Great Fire of London in 1666 the idea of insuring against fire had been born and companies offering such insurance had first appeared the following year. In spite of the devastation and privation caused by the Great Fire an *'Act for the Prevention and Suppressing of Fires Within the City of London and the Liberties Thereof'* made certain provisions for the fighting of future fires but stopped short of forming organised bodies of men into fire brigades.

The insurers however, hard-headed business men that they were, soon realised that more must be done to prevent the destruction of their risks by fire and causing them to pay out large sums. They advertised that they had men who would fight fires at insured property, taking pains to extol the capabilities of such men in such actions. Not only did they supply the fire fighters but they supplied the fire fighting equipment, thereby creating fire brigades for the first time since the Roman era. One of the great benefits accruing from the provision of equipment was that fire engines began to be developed and improved at a greater rate than ever before.

When anyone took out a fire insurance they then came under the protection of the private fire brigade of whichever insurance company they were with, although initially they were only available in large cities. A plate bearing that company's logo, called a firemark, would be affixed to the insured building as proof and identification of protective cover. Should that building suffer a fire, and should it be rapidly and efficiently doused by the relevant brigade, less damage would be done, less would have to be paid out by the insurer, and less inconvenience would be caused to the insured than if the premises were severely damaged or even burned to the ground. Similarly, the protection offered by the Insurance Company's fire brigade was an incentive to buy their insurance, so adding to company profitability. The oldest known firemark is one from 1683 belonging to the Friendly Society of London.

The nearest of these privately formed insurance brigades to the Borough of Reigate was in South London. The closest other local fire brigades were in Dorking and Croydon. Due to the Borough's distance from London it seems that anyone in the Redhill or Reigate locality taking out fire insurance would have to depend on the local brigade, perhaps with assistance from a neighbouring one, and certainly not on an insurance company's force. (In 1901 the Croydon Brigade sent a horse-drawn steamer to assist at Nicol's fire in Redhill. The distance and strain of the gallop caused one of the horses involved to drop dead in its traces on arrival).

The incentive for the local brigade to deal with a fire at insured premises would not have been diminished, for having dealt with such a fire it would endeavour to recover expenses from the insuring company. Where there existed both forces - a local brigade as well as an insurance brigade (which was never the case in Reigate) the rule initially laid down by the insurance companies was that their force tackled only their customer's fires. This was later changed and they dealt with any fire they were called to and inter-brigade assistance was developed.

If the property were uninsured then costs would be recovered from the owner, not always an easy matter, and the forces of the law would sometimes have to be resorted to. This procedure continued until 1891 when it ceased, presumably the rates covering the costs as local taxes still do today.

Insurance Fireman 1810

1853-1870 - Local Insurance Agents

For a while fire insurance was sold directly by the insurance companies themselves but later local agents began to spring up. These were men normally having established business interests in an area who took on the agency for additional income.

Early entries in the records of the Sun Fire Office show the following payments: -

May 3rd 1739	*Benj. Glassbrook, Reigate*	£4.5s.0d
May 10th 1739	*William Mascall, Reigate*	£78.1s.9d

These payments are likely to have been for the same incident and may or may not have involved a local agent. One significant point about them is that they pre-date any other facts found in research, and highlights the fact that the records of a private company have survived where local manor records have not.

We have to move forward a few years to find records of fire agents locally: -

Imperial Fire Office	*28 March 1804*	*Mr Thos. Gale, Reigate, Surrey*	*Agent*
Union Fire Office	*9 July 1806*	*Mr Thos. Gale, Reigate, Surrey*	*Agent*
Union Fire Office	*3 Sept 1806*	*Mr John Westwood, Reigate, District Surveyor,*	
Northern Union Fire Office	*17 Dec 1821*	*New Reigate Agent John Brewer, Grocer & Tea Dealer and the Clerk of the Bench of that town.*	
Royal Exchange	*6 Apr 1829*	*William Moore of Reigate, requesting on account of his advanced age to resign agency in favour of his relation Mr George Morrison of the town. Accepted. Morrison appointed.*	

The above shows something about those who were in the fire insurance market. Little is known about them other than the facts shown but much more is known about a later agent in the Borough, Mr John Lees, who had an office at Reigate. He sold his first fire insurance as agent for the Westminster Fire Office on 10th February 1853. His customer on that date was one Morland Thomas of London Lane, Reigate. That gentleman had £1,200 worth of insurance at a rate of 1/6d per £100, incurring an annual premium of 36/- per annum, half of which was the Insurer's charges, the other half was tax. Rates varied to reflect the risk according to the type of premises and their usage. John Lees sold insurance cover on the 6th May 1853 to Richard Miller of Merstham and the policy book records shows: -

Cowshed and stable	*£30*
Slaughter house	*£10*
Granary	*£20*
Household goods, books, wearing apparel, watches, jewels, wine and liquors in dwelling house 'The Railway' tavern	<u>*£140*</u>
Total	*£200 Rate 3/6d*

Other rates applied per £100 insured were:

> *Shop and contents 2/-*
> *Coach house with small gas ring 2/6*
> *Haystack 5/-*
> *Pictures, paints and drawings 4/6*
> *China, glass and pottery 4/6*
> *Business with 15 men 7/6*
> *Slaughter house with live and dead stock 5/-*

From the above it can be seen that the risk grew as the item's susceptibility to fire increased, which is no more than might be expected. Bricks and mortar were at the lower end of the scale whereas easily destructible and fragile items were towards the top end. Similarly, premises with greater numbers of people in them were also more susceptible and were rated accordingly. Haystacks, whilst flammable items, were vulnerable from self-combustion if the stacked material was not properly dried, could be struck by lightening and were vulnerable to fire applied by malicious persons, and so were also rated highly. Malicious persons could be anyone, from persons holding a grudge against the stack owner to purely wanton fire raisers. From the early 1800s, and especially around 1830, there had been a huge amount of arson in connection with unrest surrounding the bringing of machinery into agriculture. Surrey suffered particularly, and there had been riots at Dorking and Guildford entailing the use of mounted troops with sabres. Arson, especially following the invention of matches, was an easy way for the people to strike back (no pun intended).

Fire insurance was big business, and even after these turbulent times the rates in force were clearly seen by many as value for money, or at least affordable when the possibility of sudden uninsured loss was considered by the owner. As well as many private houses, premises insured included many of the public houses of the time. Insured via John Lees' agency were the Somers Arms in Linkfield Street in 1854; the Sussex Arms in Redhill and the Brickmakers Arms in Sots Hole (now Kings Avenue) Redhill in 1857; the White Hart Hotel, Reigate, in 1858; the Castle beer shop in 1860 and the Prince of Wales in Nutley Lane in 1864.

New buildings were often insured before completion so that an investment was protected from the very beginning. The Reigate Public Hall was insured in the course of erection in 1861, as was the Star public house in 1867. (Insurance of the latter at such an early stage turned out to be a little ironic as in October of 1896 proceedings had to be instigated against the keeper of the Star Public House to recover expenses incurred by the Redhill Brigade in putting out a fire there). The Building Committee of the Reigate and Redhill Cottage Hospital also ensured that its responsibilities were met by insuring *'upon building of Cottage Hospital adjacent to Redhill Common at present in course of erection'* in the sum of £1,782 in 1870. Contents of such new buildings could be added to the insurance at a later date.

Although the instances above are all local to the Borough of Reigate, as befits a history on that area, John Lees activities extended far beyond its boundaries to such diverse places as Dorking, London, Sussex and Devon. It is also worth noting that it was a John Lees who presided over the 1862 meeting to buy a new fire engine. (As the business of John Lees, the fire insurance agent, clearly depended on an efficient fire fighting force it would seem safe to assume the names referred to one and the same person).

The Westminster Fire Insurance Company was one of a number of such companies that came to operate in the Borough. The Norwich Union Office had its agents, Wilson and Cleather, established in Station Road, Redhill, and in later years one of their clients was the tailors, Pratt Bros. of London Road, Redhill. A fire occurred at their premises one night and before the fire brigade arrived a crowd had broken the windows. The fire was duly extinguished but the newspaper account stated that *'considerable damage was done, both upstairs and down, by the unnecessary use of water. Fortunately the damage is fully covered.....'*

Incidentally, if it is wondered if the premises of local fire agents ever caught fire - and if they did were they insured - then the answer in at least one case is yes. On September 29th, 1902, a gas ring overheated laths in the basement ceiling of 13 High Street, Reigate in spite of it being protected by iron plate. The owner of the premises was Frank Weller, the agent for the County Fire Office. There was an estimated £1.10.0 worth of damage which he had covered by his company's insurance.

Other Insurance Offices in Reigate and Redhill

Year	*Name of Insurance Office*	*Name and address of Agent*
1903	The Royal Insurance Office	Mr G.Johnson, High St., Reigate
1903	Unknown	Mr Ingram Selwyn, Bell St., Reigate
1908	Sun	Mr J.W.B.Northover, Bell St., Reigate
1909	County Fire Office	Mr H.R. Gillham, Waterside, Redhill [5]

1864-1869 - Insurance Tax

At one of the very early Reigate Borough Council meetings, that of 14th March 1864 (the first ever meeting was on the 9th December 1863) the first item on the agenda was; *'To consider an application from the Society for the Abolition or Reduction of the Duty on Fire Insurances touching a proposed petition to Parliament from the Corporation, and to take measures thereupon.'* The minutes do not enlighten us as to what discussion took place, merely recording that: *'The Town Clerk read out the petition engrossed. Councillor Young proposed that it receive the common seal and be prepared for transmission.'* The proposition was: *'Resolved in the affirmative.'* This subject was to receive many airings at Reigate Borough Council meetings, and in December 1866, two and a half years later, there was again a petition affixed with the Borough's common seal and forwarded to Parliament.

The reason for the petitions was resistance to the tax on fire insurance that had first been levied in 1782. Although the rate varied over the years it was around 1/6d per £100 insured. As we have already seen, the premium for a dwelling house was also 1/6d, so the amount payable was doubled by the tax, making the calls for its abolition understandable. Insurance companies must have seen it as a device to make people think twice about fire insurance and deter many from taking it up at all. They, along with councils from all over the country, exerted considerable pressure on the Government, eventually successfully so, for the tax was abolished in 1869. The irony of the matter is that we now once again have a tax on insurance imposed in 1995 by the Conservative government of the time.

Notes to Chapter Two

[1] *Another point of Fred Legg's that it would be nice to be able to fully corroborate is that the Reigate Brigade had been re-formed in 1864 under a Captain. Watch Committee records of 1866 reveal that the Redhill Brigade had the Superintendent rank and it is probable that Job Heath Apted at Reigate had the same title. It may have been that Fred Legg, in his history, used the word Captaincy as there had been Captains in his day and it was easier than using the term 'Superintendency'. The situation is further compounded by the same Watch Committee records noting, in April of 1867, the resignation of Job H. Apted as Inspector of the Western Ward Fire Brigade. More is made of this under heading 'Job Heath Apted' on page 20.*

[2] *Perhaps he too had been a previous Inspector of Lighting.*

[3] *In Alan Ingram's book 'Social Scenes of Yesterday' there is a 1907 picture of the Redhill manual appliance, complete with crew, and a caption stating that the engine of the 'B' district (Redhill) was built in 1865. The same caption also states that the engine of 'A' district (Reigate) was built in 1857. Confirmation of the above dates comes from the 1912 report to the Watch Committee by Major Gerald C.M.Rouse, the then Chief Fire Officer. In that report he made the remarks: 'Both manuals have had to be repaired on several occasions. The manual in 'A' district was built in 1857 and the manual in 'B' in 1865 and both are showing the effects of age and hard work'.*

[4] *Invoice presented to Watch Committee at 1st April 1868 meeting.*

[5] *Mr Henry R. Gillham, of Waterside, Redhill, came to Redhill in 1853/4 and built houses, ran an ironmongery, set up Redhill's first baths, became a councillor, an architect and general all-round successful business man in the town.*

Chapter three
The 19th Century Draws to a Close

Other Fire Fighting Forces

Some large companies and organisations had their own fire fighting teams and equipment. One such was the Royal Philanthropic Society Farm School in Redhill. It is not known precisely when the squad was formed but it was possibly in 1870, when the sale to the school of one of the Borough's old engines in 1870 took place (see previous chapter). How effective was the use they made of it is uncertain for the Redhill Brigade was called to a fire at the Philanthropic in 1874. The situation was reversed in 1910 when the School's fire team turned up with a manual engine to assist at a fire at Trower's warehouse in St Johns Terrace Road, Earlswood. If it was the same engine it would have been at least one hundred and one years old by then.

Also having their own fire brigades were large houses. Mention is made of the Priory Private Fire Brigade in a report of the 1913 fire drill competitions held at Reigate Lodge. This is assumed to be either the Reigate Priory force or another from Nutfield Priory. It could have been either because among regular brigades competing were those of Reigate and of South Nutfield. However, it is known that Reigate Priory was also called Priory House, as after a 1904 fire at Burtenshaw's coach works a hydrant situated in Bell Street, Reigate, is referred to as being opposite Priory House. These private forces received their training from the regular brigades. A 1904 account of such training at Priory House involved three firemen who trained employees listed (slightly confusingly) as: - *'H.Simms Snr., F. Brown, Reader, Motor Man, Garden boy and two garden men'.*

The provision of hydrants made it possible for shops and companies to have their own hose pipes that they could connect and get a jet of water onto the seat of a fire on first discovery, and usually before the fire brigade arrived. Two firms who did this were the Reigate Brewery, staff from which in 1907 fought a fire at the back of the High Street shops adjacent to their premises, and nearby Northover's, whose staff fought a 1908 fire on their own premises before the arrival of the Reigate Brigade.

It seems that there were also private hydrants. One was situated 30 yards south of the Beehive beer house in Dovers Green Road, Reigate, and in a letter to the Watch Committee in 1908 Fred Legg suggested that it be taken over by the Corporation so that the fire brigade could regularly inspect it.

1893/4 - New Captain at Reigate

Mr F.Fuller had been appointed Superintendent of Reigate in 1875. At some time his rank became that of Captain but, as has been said before, the situation as regards Supt/Capt is unclear. In October of 1891 Captain Fuller resigned and in the following January 250 handbills were circulated in West Ward advertising the post. By April applications had been received from Edwin Legg, his son Fred Legg, and Mark Dean. In July of 1892 Captain Fuller was still in post and nothing seeming to be happening about replacing him. It was a situation that was to persist until November 1893 when 50 more handbills were printed again advertising the post.

By the next meeting on the 11th December there had been only one application, from Edwin Legg of Reigate. This single application must have been seen to be inadequate and the exercise was repeated in January of 1894 with the distribution of a third set of handbills. This brought forth four applications by February. In addition to Edwin Legg there was now his son, Sub-Engineer Fred Legg, and two others, Michael Whitmore and Charles Wood.

Fred Legg was the successful applicant. He had joined the brigade in 1886 and been appointed

Advert c.1881

Sub-engineer five years later in 1891. He took over as Captain with effect from March 1894 and Charles Wood was promoted to Sub-Engineer in his place. By April Fred Legg was being measured and fitted out with his new uniform.

Disadvantage and Delay

But Fred Legg and his colleagues in both forces had to contend with the all of the disadvantages of the early types of manual fire fighting appliances, including its prime mover, the horse. No doubt the animals did their best for their masters, but a delay was built in to the system by their having to be fetched and brought to the engine for harnessing before any progress was possible. If the fire was at night then additional delay was incurred, as a man would have to be roused from his bed to open up the stable and valuable time was wasted whilst the fire crew waited at the engine shed.

The horses would have come from either the local stables or a nearby farm, depending on the arrangements in force at the time and the season. In Redhill's case Marsh's Redhill stables, situated where Woolworth's is now, supplied horses for some time, as did the cab rank at the nearby railway station. This would have been a fairly good arrangement as the distance between the stables or the railway station and the fire station was short.

There is said to have been another arrangement at one time, which entailed a loud bell being fitted on top of the Market Hall in Redhill. This bell would have alerted local firemen, but it was also supposed to alert the farm at the top of Redstone Hill, from where horses would be brought down into the town. Information regarding this arrangement was related in 1996 by Mrs Wall of Bletchingley who, in her younger days, worked at the hat shop next to the Market Hall in Redhill. She heard it from the proprietor, Mr Brinley Thomas, who in the 1940s was speaking of times during *his* younger days, presumably 1900-1920-ish. [1]

There were other delays incurred in summoning the firemen. They were volunteers who had to be summoned from home or their place of work by messenger. In the very early days there was no other way, short of having a permanent force on continual standby, of expediting matters, but later fire bells, maroons or a siren could have been used. By 1897, when there was criticism in the local press of the old method still being employed, the option of telephonic communication had been added.

Nothing was done at this time, however, and four years later, in 1901, when Nicol's shop caught fire, a policeman still had to be sent by bicycle to call out the firemen. [2] By 1912 the situation regarding horses seems not to have changed. In a report of that year, already partly quoted, Major Rouse, the Chief Fire Officer said:

'The horsing arrangements are not satisfactory and there is no certainty that horses can be obtained when required. In the case of 'A' district there is no-one living over the stables and the coachman has to come from Nutley Lane. In the event of a night call valuable time is wasted, as the crew has to wait at the station for the horses to arrive. There is also delay in calling the 'E' district men in the event of a fire call as a messenger has to be sent round to each house as they are not on a bell circuit'. ('E' district was Earlswood)

The problems were not restricted to the supply of horses, they also concerned the training of the animals. This is illustrated by the following 1912 article in a local newspaper:

' "A horse! a horse! My Kingdom for a horse" whispered a well-known tradesman to me as we took stock of the turnout of the Redhill Fire Brigade on Tuesday when a summons was received from Bletchingley for their services. It was a strange sight, was that turnout. It might have terminated in a turnout of another description when "a horse" did arrive. It was a spirited animal and was intended as a leader up Redstone Hill. He evidently objected to the fuss and flurry. He did not take kindly to being hurried from his stall and being called upon the assist the pair harnessed to the engine. He raised strong

objections, and also his heels, and deliberately got down on his knees, swearing an oath in horsey language that he would see all the firemen to Jericho before he would put his shoulder in the collar. His objections were upheld, and he was unharnessed from the pole, sauntering back to his stable tossing his head like an obstinate boy, who, when chastised, pouts his lower lip in a don't care sort of manner.

'But when a fire, which is a good servant but a bad master, is blazing away, the eccentricities of a horse is not considered. The little incident should teach members of the Watch Committee a lesson. Men are trained to work a fire engine, and why not train the horses that are called upon to haul machine to the scene of the conflagration. There are some good animals in Marsh's stables, but before they are attached to a fire engine with a clanging bell, they should have some experience of the work they are called upon to perform. This is only possible by training, and unless the Watch Committee will sanction payment for the hire of horses periodically to get them accustomed to their particular work we may have other exhibitions of temper or fright. It is the first few minutes that are so important when a fire breaks out. It often means the saving of life, and often means an outbreak spreading to larger dimensions.'

The writer had been witness to a scene that might have occurred many times. How often the matter of training horses had cropped up over the years is unknown, but it must have been allied to the conception of the brigade owning its own horses. In this case they would have seen steady service in the matter of pulling the engines both in drills and real situations, and would thereby have become ideal for the task. The fact that this did not happen can most likely only have been due to the practicality of the matter, mainly, no doubt, the costs that would have been incurred. Once the brigade relied on hired horses then the idea of training a horse that might have been pulling a cart or a plough the next time a fire broke out also had its impractical side.

Having said all that there is doubt that a bell was very often fitted to a fire engine, quite possibly for the very reason of skittish horses. Bells were fitted to London engines in 1904 but they had horses that were permanently engaged in the work of pulling engines to fires, whereas the provinces did not. The absence of bells on fire engines of the time is confirmed by looking at photos of engines, and they do not show any evidence of bells being carried.

The reference to the clanging bell on the engine of the quoted newspaper article is therefore a mystery. Perhaps a bell had been fitted at the time as someone's 'good idea' that turned out to be not so good. Horses did tend to have minds of their own at times, and whatever their objections to co-operating with attempts to harness them to fire engines, it was a situation that was not to be solved until motorised vehicles did away with the problem altogether.

Not that horses were to blame all of the time. Often they were expected to perform to their maximum ability, and no greater effort was expected from them when they were asked to gallop all the way to a fire. The problem with this was that the distances varied from fire to fire, the weather was not always conducive of fast travel, and the terrain was certainly hostile to a horse's efforts to drag a heavy engine up and down dale on rough roads. This was a fact recognised by Fred Legg in May 1900 when he wrote the following to the Borough Council.

'Gentlemen, I have been asked by Capt. J. Mason to express to you my views with regard to having an extra conveyance for out district fires, I am of the opinion that an extra conveyance should be had and it should be left to the discretion of the officers in charge. Mr Nash White Hart will supply Van Horse & Man for 17/6d. I consider this a fair charge. I may add, in proof of the necessity of an extra conveyance, that a 6-inch manual like the Reigate Engine, when fully equipped & with 8 men & driver, weighs about 2 tons. We now carry 11 men & driver besides extra hose etc., so, Gentlemen - you can quite see how difficult it is to maintain a good gallop with 2 horses, I also consider the extra conveyance should be had, if considered necessary, by the Officer-in-Charge for attending fires in Redhill, or visi-versa, as you then get a long gallop, & of course speed is of first importance. In most towns a Tender usually follows the engine but the extra conveyance amounts to the same thing.

I am Gentlemen Yours Respectfully F. Legg Capt. R.F.B.'
There is no record of this letter being brought to the attention of the Watch Committee but as it is addressed to the members of the Council perhaps it was dealt with at full council meeting. [3] It is a fact that today the idea of additional transport is one that is taken up for a variety of reasons.

1894 - Brigade Insurance
The subject of insuring property against fire has already been dealt with but fighting fires is a hazardous business for the men who, at a moments notice, rush with all speed to the latest conflagration, knowing not what they may encounter there. They apply their efforts and skills to the job at hand with a vigour that can all too easily be turned to sudden, painful injury if things go wrong. Too many firemen have been injured through the course of their duties, and too many have lost their lives subjecting themselves to the dangers that lurk at all fires.
Insuring firemen and their equipment has been common practice for many years. In the 1890s it was the London Accident and Guarantee Company that provided the necessary cover for the Corporation's fire department, and payments were made to the Redhill Captain in 1896, and the following year for an accident to fireman Charles Winchester.

Out Stations
It is known that out-stations existed in 1897 at South Park, Meadvale and Earlswood as the respective Captains of Reigate and Redhill were asking for new equipment for them. The precise date of their individual establishments is uncertain, but known information is as follows:

MEADVALE
In September 1903 hoses were moved to Mr Woodman's premises in Somerset Road. Rent was fixed at 1/- per week.
In the summer of 1913 a coach house in Somerset Road was rented from Mr Heasman.

SOUTH PARK
The earliest mention of fire fighting premises at South Park is in 1885 when Watch Committee minutes refer to a stand pipe and 100 feet of hose being obtained for it. Equipment at the South Park station was the subject of a letter from the Reigate Captain, Fred Legg, in July 1897. He was asking for the renewal of 120 ft of 2½ inch, 40 year-old leather hose and the provision of a cart to carry 600 ft of hose as well as tools ladders and other equipment. With a view to having his request acceded to he pointed out that manufacture of the cart by local firm G. Burtenshaw of West Street, Reigate, would save £4 over other manufactures, costing only £9-£10 rather than £14. Further savings would be made by the re-use of the old unions and a 4 foot 8 inch branch pipe being returned to Reigate as too large for use on cottages. He suggested that the truck be sited at Mr M.Crust's premises at a rent of £2 12 per annum. Mr Crust was also Foreman Crust at Reigate. He had a wheelwright's business at 78 Priory Road in South Park (as it is not believed he had moved to Allingham Road at that time) and had working for him his son, Ernest Crust. Fred Legg also suggested that the son be appointed a reserve fireman at South Park.
As far as the request for equipment is concerned, all the sub stations had their equipment upgraded at a cost of around £150.
In January, 1910, the Watch Committee decided to acquire new fire premises at South Park. A Mr F.Bush was to provide a new building at £5/annum and the old to be vacated as soon as the new was ready. This idea either fell through or was not agreed by full council, for within weeks Mr M.Crust of South Park was asking for increased rent for the storage of the fire appliances and Chief

Officer Rouse (more about him later) was submitting plans for a new fire station to be built on a council depot at South Park. This plan was not approved, however, and the whole matter was put into abeyance for twelve months. At the suggestion of the Chief Officer a shed was rented next to the Holmesdale Inn at a rent of £3.3.0 per annum and notice was given by the Council to Mr Crust for the Fire Brigade to quit his premises, used up to this time as the fire station.

EARLSWOOD
In September 1903 hoses were moved to Mr Goss's premises in Common Road.

1897 - Suggestions for Change
Fred Legg had an idea for an extension to the Reigate fire station in the form of a reading room cum storeroom. He felt that if it were made reasonably attractive to the men to be there in the evenings then they would already be on site if a fire call were to be received. The problem of having to return home for a uniform would be overcome by the provision of a cupboard in which spare uniforms could be kept, also handy in cases when men were working nearer the station than their home when a call came. He explained to the gentleman of the Watch Committee in a letter that his motive was to do everything possible to improve turn-out times, adding that such a room should be a part of every new fire station. With the provision of a new station at Reigate only four years away perhaps this last remark was particularly timely.

1897 - A Steamer
The local press had, in 1897, expressed the opinion that the time had come for the acquisition of a 'steamer', a horse-drawn fire engine on which steam power, rather than muscle power, was used to pump water from a nearby supply to quench whatever flames might present themselves. The press quoted surrounding boroughs that had decided steamers were well worth the £500 they cost to buy. Dorking had recently taken delivery of a Merryweather engine, and Tunbridge Wells had two steamers. Guildford also bought a steamer in this year of 1897.

There had been an enquiry by the Fire Appliances Manufacturing Company about the possible demonstration of a steam engine as early as August-September 1892, but this had been declined. There was, however, a trial of a Merryweather steamer conducted on Saturday 13th November 1897 in the Market Field at Redhill. Evidence of this trial was supplied in 1964 by Mr Frederick Winchester, then aged 71, who had been a fireman from 1911 to 1936. His father, Mr Charles Winchester, a volunteer fireman at the time of the trial, was directly involved and he and his son Frederick, then aged 5 or 6, took wood along to get the fire going and boil the water in the steamer.

The water required to test the pumping efficiency of the machine was, Mr Winchester presumed, drawn by hose from the Redhill Brook. This is quite probable, the brook was more forceful than it is today and the machine could have been positioned within the required fifteen feet of it. Its presence could well have been one of the reasons why that site was chosen for the demonstration, others being that it was centrally placed in the town and there was plenty of room.

Mr Francis Barnes was the new Mayor and Chairman of the Watch Committee at this time. He had been a member of the Council only six years when he succeeded Henry Ongley in November 1897. He was a tradesman, a man of means, son and business inheritor of the first importer of Danish bacon to this country, and he lived in considerable style at Reigate Heath. It was his duty to report to the Committee about the trial of the steamer at which he had been present. His report was delivered verbally and it is not known precisely what was said. What is known is that it was generally contended that connection to the Caterham Water Company's mains provided all the pressure that was required to supply the hoses with efficient jets, and in the places where mains

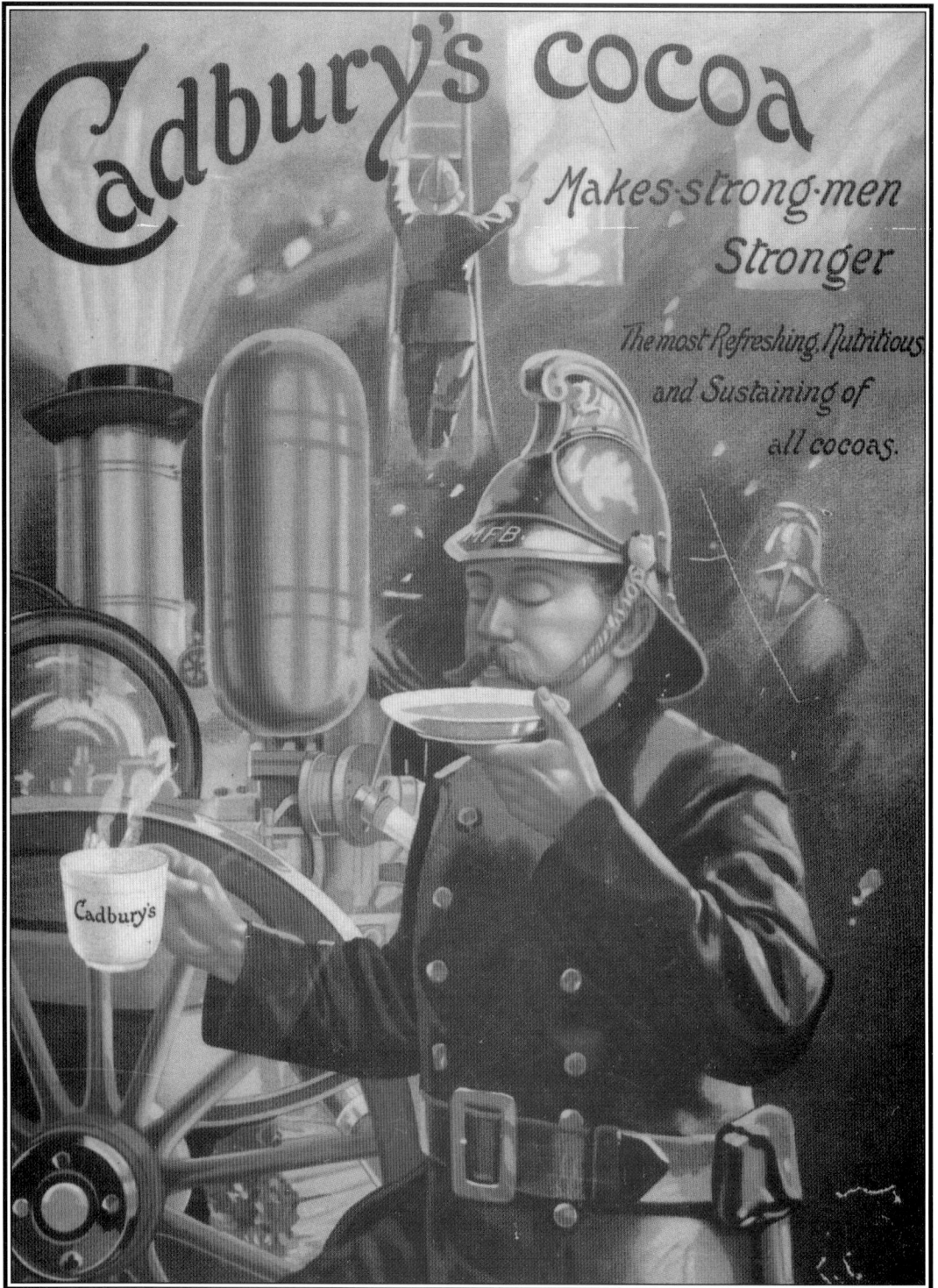

The fire engine featured in this c1890 advertisement is of the steam powered type

did not exist the manual pump could draw water from a local stream or pond and this would suffice. The result was that Reigate never did buy a steamer. The exhibition steamer was returned to the maker with no sale in prospect.

A photo of the steamer was taken - Mr Winchester had a copy but it was in poor condition - and in it were included a number of firemen of the day. Apart from Mr Charles Winchester these were said to be Senior Superintendent Jack Mason and firemen Charlwood, Vosper, Hockett and Roberts. In fact Jack, or John, Mason was a foreman at Redhill and H.Charlwood was the Captain at the time.

In spite of the decision not to buy a steamer, such a machine had advantages that at least one of the two Captains desired. After a fire on September 12th, 1903, at Littleton Farm, Reigate, F.Legg was to again ask the Watch Committee for a steamer because there had been only 5 men available locally to pump the manual engine, his own men having to do some of this work. In spite of this request Reigate never did make the purchase.

1897 - Brigade Strength
At this time the strength of the Western Ward force was nine men but it was proposed to increase the strength to 12 men plus the Captain. This was achieved by the addition of new men Frederick Mackrell, Ernest Crust and Frank Smith. Two men were about to retire, however. One of these was Forman Martin Crust, 53 years old, father of Ernest Crust and past the normal retirement age, and even older, at 56, another Reigate man, Engineer Edwin Legg, father of the current Reigate Captain. It was this Captain, Fred Legg, who wrote to the Watch Committee asking that the services of both men be extended for three more years. That their services must have been valued, at least by not having to recruit new but raw talent, was proved by the granting of this request in the October of that year.

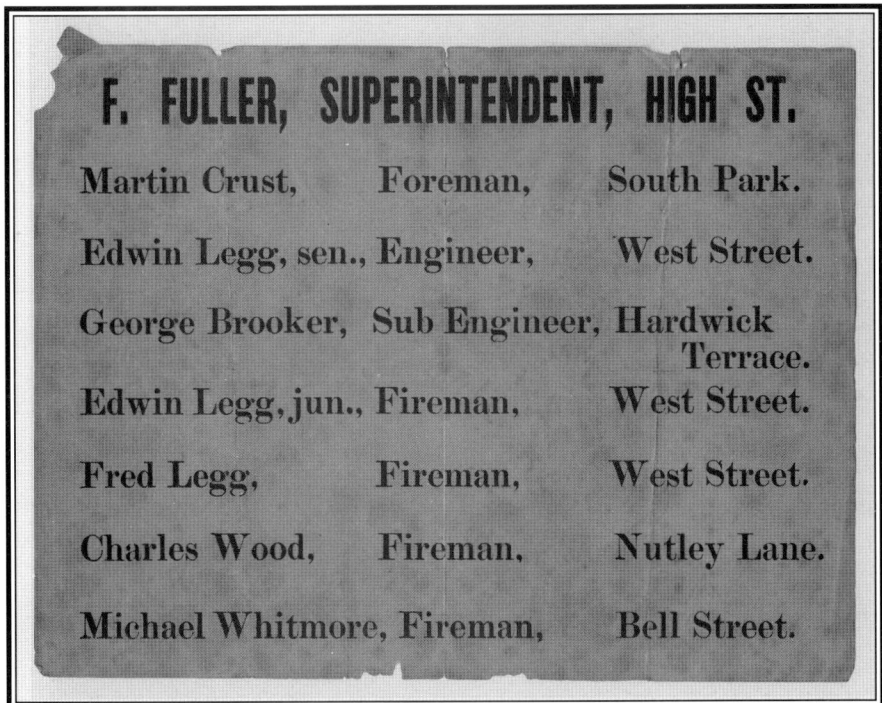

F. FULLER, SUPERINTENDENT, HIGH ST.

Martin Crust, Foreman, South Park.

Edwin Legg, sen., Engineer, West Street.

George Brooker, Sub Engineer, Hardwick Terrace.

Edwin Legg, jun., Fireman, West Street.

Fred Legg, Fireman, West Street.

Charles Wood, Fireman, Nutley Lane.

Michael Whitmore, Fireman, Bell Street.

Early list of Brigade members

BOROUGH OF REIGATE.

WESTERN   FIRE

WARD   BRIGADE,

❧ REIGATE. ☙

F. Legg,	Captain,	West Street.
M. Crust,	Foreman,	South Park.
E. Legg,	Engineer,	Little West St.
C. Wood,	Sub-Engineer,	York Road.
M. Whitmore,	Fireman,	Hardwick Terrace.
W. Wood,	Fireman,	Nutley Lane.
W. Powell,	Fireman,	South Albert Rd.
T. Whitmore,	Fireman,	Nutley Lane.
W. Wells,	Fireman,	North Albert Rd.
H. Sandell,	Reserve,	Bell Street.
A. Cork,	Messenger,	Little West Street.
G. Bennet,	Messenger,	High Street.

N.B.--In case of Fire the alarm to be given at the Police Station.

Early list of members updated

1897-1903 - Uniforms

Redhill and Reigate Fire Brigade uniforms were not entirely standard because piecemeal ordering resulted in some men's uniforms being different from others. An attempt to correct this was made in 1897 when Captain Fred Legg asked for a complete set of new uniforms and belts for the Western Ward Brigade so that standardisation could be achieved.

Surprisingly, his own uniform differed from that of his men to the point whereby he was also asking for head protection for himself. He explained that he had had several near misses from falling tiles. He also wanted his helmet, assuming it was provided, to be of white metal, along with epaulettes the same, so his rank was apparent at nighttime.

This request was one that applied to Redhill as well as to Reigate men and the whole Brigade was measured by the Shand Mason representative on September 17th 1898, and supplied on November 4th of that year with new uniforms by that company.

The Legg family of Reigate fire fighters, 1924. Fred Legg is pictured second from left with his three sons (from L-R) John, George and Fred (Sherry)

The specification of the uniforms was impressive. For the Reigate men there were thirteen full dress uniforms of good, serviceable black cloth similar to those worn in the Metropolitan Brigade. Each had a double-breasted tunic with a red patch either side of the collar, red piping on the edges of the cloth, belt support hooks, four pockets and 12 buttons. The only exception was that the Captain's buttons were silver plated. The trousers had red piping down the outside seams, side and watch pockets. Caps had red piping and the letters RCfB masked in red. Four additional brass helmets were supplied as well as a white metal one for the Captain. He also got his white metal epaulettes. Also supplied were 12 leather waist belts, 13 pairs of waterproof boots, 11 japanned hand lamps, 4 pocket lines with loops and spring hooks, 5 hand axes, 5 leather pouches to keep them in, 10 hose wrenches with pouches, and last of all, 12 enamelled nameplates marked 'FIREMAN'.

The whole of the above was priced at £52-5s.

Redhill men got the same, in different quantities of course. There were also uniforms for Earlswood and Meadvale men, although no mention of South Park personnel - perhaps they were included in the Reigate equipment.

It would be interesting to know how the men received the new clothing. Were they pleased? - excited even? - proud? As most of them were volunteers it is assumed that at least they felt they were being recognised and clothed with a certain amount of status.

And the price! The entire Corporation Brigade cloth in best dress uniforms for something not too much over £100! Just to think how much some of those items might cost to buy today, around 100 years later - and how much some might fetch were they for sale in the right place today!

The uniforms were expected to last for five years, and in October 1903 Fred Legg was again writing in for new uniforms for all the Reigate men. Thirteen sets plus 2 axes, 2 handlamps, 3 whistles and chains and 1 pair of wire cutters were supplied by Shand and Mason on December 5th. [4]

A New Captain at Redhill

In 1899 John Mason was the acting Captain at Redhill. Captain Charlwood, for reasons that are unclear, was unable to continue to carry out his duties and resigned in the September of 1899, John Mason being promoted Captain in his place.

1899 - Reigate Engine Worn Out

Letter from Fred Legg, Captain of Reigate Brigade, August 21st 1899:

To his Worship the Mayor and Gentlemen of the Watch Committee.

I beg to report that the pumps and valves of the Reigate Fire Engine require new leathering and thorough overhauling. The engine leaks and also draws air and therefore does not throw but half the quantity it should. I find the engine is now 42 years old and I understand very little has been done to it intentionally in that time. I am of the opinion that the time has come when we should have a new engine but that could wait until we have a suitable Fire Station. In the meantime I would suggest that the present engine be thoroughly overhauled and that an order be given to the makers, Shand Mason & Co., to do so at once as I fear that should we get a heavy fire at which the engine would be required to throw water she might break down.

I am Gentlemen, yours respectfully, F.Legg.

Letter from Shand Mason Co. to F. Legg Esq. Captain Reigate Fire Brigade, Aug. 25th 1899

Upper Ground Street, Blackfriars Road, London S.E.

Dear Sir,

Referring to the interview our representative had with you we beg to estimate.

To thoroughly overhaul your fire engine, to take the same to pieces and repair the works, supply a new set of leather cups to the plungers, take out valves - surface and refix to places, supply and fix new leather joints to the valve box, supply all necessary iron joints and pins to slings and guides and refit to place, supply a new set of springs to levers and refix 1 ladder bracket.

We undertake to carry out the work and send a competent engineer to Reigate, it being understood that you give him the assistants (sic) of one man for the sum of £10.

At the same time we wish to call your attention to the fact that this engine, which was supplied by us in 1857, should be sent here and thoroughly overhauled, the above repairs executed, and in addition the whole of the wood work to be cleaned and scraped and carefully repainted in 6 coats of best oil colour finish in vermilion, and written in gold letters shaded 'Reigate'. When this is done the engine would be quite equal to new. The cost of this work complete would be £35-0-0.

This price includes the cost of loan of a replacement engine while yours is away.

Awaiting the favour of your esteemed instruction which shall have our best and prompt attention in all respects, we are yours Truly, Shand Mason & Co.

Letter from the Mayor to Fred Legg.

Normanton
Reigate
Aug. 28th 1899

Dear Sir

The Committee authorise an expenditure on the Engine of £10, so you can ask Shand mason to do the repairs. I think it wise not to do more as we may get a new Engine.

Yours Truly,
F.E.Barnes

Unaddressed, undated and enthusiastic letter from Fred Legg.

Shand Mason engineer new leathered the whole of valve box and connections and fitted new cups to plungers and tested the Engine with water supplied from the hydrant situated opposite the Public Hall and the Engine threw 2 x ⅞ jet of water clean over the tower of the Congregational Church.

F.Legg, Captain.

These letters are important because they answer questions pending, in effect, for 42 years. Those questions were:

Was a new engine definitely supplied in 1857?   Answer: Yes

If so, who was the manufacturer?   Answer: Shand Mason

They also confirm that the reason for the different entries in the Churchwardens records of the late 1850s was due to the supply of the new engine, although the actual information is lacking from them.

Also the details of the repairs tell us more about the engine. The style of the letters themselves add to the feel of the times, taking out some of the otherwise bland approach to what was essentially a straightforward business transaction between two parties.

Notes for Chapter Three

[1] *Mr Brinley Thomas had a second Redhill hat shop on the corner of High Street and Rees Road.*

[2] *Except for the captains of the Redhill and Reigate Brigades who, by chance, both happened to be in Redhill town at the time.*

[3] *Full Council minutes for this period not consulted.*

[4] *Source: Fred Legg's Reports and Applications book for 1903.*

Chapter Four
A New Century

Nicol's Fire and Escape Ladder Sales

The Twentieth Century started badly with a disastrous fire at Nicol's shop in Redhill in May of 1901, in which two assistants lost their lives (see illustration p123). Details of this, one of the most notable and documented fires ever to occur in Reigate Borough, are given elsewhere.

There might have been some embarrassment in the Borough in December of that same year following the offer of an old escape ladder to the Horley Parish Council. It was a hand drawn ladder from Redhill station that had been used at the Nicol's fire and was old and due for replacement. A problem was that the ladder makers would make no offer for the old escape in order to defray £80 cost of its replacement. The Watch Committee therefore advised the Reigate Town Clerk to approach Horley with the offer. The embarrassment arose when this offer was not only rejected but done so publicly and in terms which poured considerable scorn upon the fact that the offer had been made at all.

The vehicle for this rejection was a letter in the Surrey Mirror written by the Captain of the Horley Brigade, Captain E.W.Jenkins. He wrote: - *'I was very much amused......in which they* (the Reigate Town Council) *proposed to get rid of their old ladder. Horley and its fire appliances are, perhaps, a little more up-to-date than the members of the Reigate Town Council give them credit for, and as there is not in Horley a museum for the housing of relics of antiquity, I suggest the Reigate authorities keep their old fire escape and build a home in their own town to receive it.'*

This was pretty strong stuff, certainly not something to be misunderstood - Horley was clearly not prepared to become Reigate Borough's dumping ground. Captain Jenkins went on to suggest that better still, the ladder be converted into a water tower, something the Redhill Captain might have found very useful for commanding the roofs of Nicol's shop and the Wheatsheaf Hotel at the recent town centre fire. It is noted from Watch Committee records that an old fire escape was sold to the Earlswood Asylum in 1913 for £5. Whether this was *the* ladder is uncertain, but given the twelve year delay it seems unlikely. Back in 1901, the purchase of a new escape ladder (and the possible riddance of the old one by whatever means) probably took place.

If this signalled change at Redhill then the building of the Municipal Buildings at Castlefield Road, Reigate, in 1901, with a fire station incorporated in the new structure, signalled even greater change. The new station officially opened the following year but in September 1903 there was what seems a rather surprising letter written by Fred Legg, again concerning a ladder, to the members of the Reigate Council Finance Committee; viz:

'Gentlemen, I ask your permission to use the new 40ft ladder, which is at present housed in the fire station, should the necessity arise, and also to acquaint my men with the method of raising the ladder. Trusting you will grant me this favour, Yours Respectfully, etc....'

What was the ladder for if not to be used? How was it to be used if the men were not acquainted with it? Perhaps there is more to this matter than meets the eye - certainly it was unusual for the letter to be addressed to the Finance Committee - maybe there's a clue there - but permission was granted in the same month. [1]

The Isolation Hospital

The Isolation Hospital opened in 1901 and Mark Dean, a member of its committee, recalled that when discussing fire precautions it was suggested that both the Redhill and Reigate Brigades should be called to see which could do the journey to Whitebushes on Three Arch Road in the shortest time. This was done and each Brigade timed from the moment of the telephone call. The Reigate Brigade was the quickest by three minutes, but Mark Dean does not go on to say if procedure in case of fire was to always call the Reigate Brigade first, or whether to always call both Brigades. It seems that various factors could govern the speed of response and cause quite considerable variations in response times.

While the two Brigades were on site during that first test call it was decided to try the fire hydrant and see how it worked. There was only one and it was situated in the centre of the block of buildings. It was a fortunate the test was made for the supply was via a meter with only an inch pipe. The surveyor was contacted and things were soon corrected, with the central hydrant being made adequate for the task and a second hydrant being connected at the entrance to supply the

Early fire fighting methods in the home.
adjoining hospital belonging to the Reigate Rural Council.

1892-1907 - Inventory of Equipment
The following list of equipment at Reigate was made out in 1892 and checked each year up to 1907 when one oil can was found to be missing. It might make interesting reading for some readers but for others be a part of this history to skip, but for completeness is included here. It was written in

the front of a report book kept by Fred Legg.

1 Manual Engine
1 Hose Reel
1 Escape and canvas shute
10 Ladders - *2 sent to South Park in 1898*
1 Fire hook
1700 ft Canvas hose
160 ft 2½ inch leather hose
200 ft 1½ inch leather hose
6 lengths suction pipe
1 jumping sheet
1 life belt and line and pulley wheel
2 coils of life line - *1 broken June 14th 1897 at Pitt's fire.*
2 engine lamps
2 lanterns
3 Hydrants
1 Skeleton hydrant
1 suction basket and strap
12 new leather buckets
12 old leather buckets - *very bad in 1902*
1 canvas dam
1 length india rubber hose for tap
1 grease jack
1 long screwdriver and iron handle
4 branch pipes
1 suction strainer
2 breeching pieces
2 Prossers patent nozzles
9 nozzles various sizes
1 fan spreader
1 screw wrench
1 clawed hammer
4 hose clips
1 hose bandage
2 ladder hooks
20 arm straps for helpers
2 brooms
1 dusting brush
2 wash leathers
1 oil can
2 scrubbing brushes
1 spoke brush
1 sponge
2 oil brushes
2 oil cans
4 tin oil bottles

1 stool
1 fire shovel
2 hydrant wrenches
1 spade
1 crow bar
1 pick & handle
1 saw
4 water keys
500ft new canvas hose & swivel lugs to couplings
    from Shand & Mason
800 ft canvas hose - rcvd from Rose & Co.
    in 1898 for South Park (2 ladders sent to South Park)
1 new stand pipe, 4 nozzles 1 branch, 2 L hooks
    from Shand & Mason Oct 1st 1899
Hose truck & 200 ft canvas hose taken to South Park Nov 25th 1899
1000 ft $2_{1/2}$ canvas hose in 10 lengths & swivel couplings
    from Shand and Mason Jan 8th 1902
Engine returned same date
3 bright steel sway bars
1 stand pipe - 1 set of keys
1 Branching - 1 set double connectors
4 nozzles - 2 branch pipes Merryweather Jan 1902

No hand pumps appear on the above list. These items were first procured for the two Brigades in 1904. Extinguishers do not appear either; the first mention of these was in February 1909 when two of *'Digg's patent chemical fire extinguishers, Brigade pattern, solid copper body trimmed inside, capacity three gallons,'* were to be purchased at £5.10.0 each, one for Redhill, one for Reigate.

The same book that contained the above items also listed events and the men present at each. The events included engine drill, escape drill, fire plug drill, the cleaning of engine and appliances and ladder drill. These occurred during three-month periods after which the cycle started over again. These entries go on unchanged until fireplug cleaning at South Park is an additional activity in October 28th, 1897. This is followed on November 13th, 1897 by the Steamer Exhibition at Redhill and, on December 20th, a maroons and plug drill. Thereafter drills are performed less often, with fireplug visits (including those at South Park) and cleaning, coupled with engine cleaning, being the main activities. The last reference to fire plugs is in 1899 when the word 'hydrants' is substituted. The testing of the hydrants in the Municipal Buildings was added in 1902.

1902 - A New Reigate Station

The new fire station was large in comparison with the old High Street station. It had a three bay engine room with doors leading out onto a short forecourt and thence directly onto Castlefield Road. It also had a cleaning room, offices and recreation room with quarters above for resident firemen. Castlefield Road was a new thoroughfare, made to serve the new and prestigious Council offices. It served the fire station well, situated fairly centrally in the Borough as it was then, with immediate access to roads to all parts.

Although the new fire station was reasonably well situated the site of the new municipal structure as a whole was a controversial one. This was because principally it was the offices of the Council for the Borough, which meant not only Reigate but Redhill as well, and many people

Laying the foundation stone of the new Reigate Fire Station.

thought that the new building should have been more centrally situated at or near Shaws Corner. Some even felt it should have been at Redhill because the eastern town had by this time outgrown its western neighbour, and if they had prevailed it would have been the Redhill Brigade getting a new station 31 years earlier than it actually did.

Land had been available at Shaws Corner but it was rejected in favour of the Castle Fields site for various reasons. It was bought at well below the going rate from Lady Henry Somerset and the votes of Reigate Councillors consistently outnumbered those of the Redhill Councillors by virtue of an inequality in the political balance of the day, whereby Reigate had more representation in Council chamber than Redhill. This resulted in the Municipal Buildings being sited at Reigate, complete with new station, and at Redhill the fire premises remained unaltered and inadequate at the back of the Market Hall.

1902-3 - Bells in Firemen's Houses

On February 9th, 1901, at Mr J.T.Peat's premises, Bell Street, Reigate, a back bedroom was burnt out. Although the Reigate Brigade arrived promptly and prevented more serious damage two of their number were not called, an omission that had Fred Legg writing in his report that electric bells ought to be considered for use once the new station at Reigate was brought into use.

The idea of fitting bells in firemen's houses was not a new one and the thorny subject of calling out firemen has already discussed in previous chapters. The technology necessary had been around for many years but it had not been until October 1897 that the question had been first raised. The suggestion was that bell circuits should be run from the police station to call out the firemen. The National Telephone Company was to be asked to provide them at a cost of £1 per bell on a five year agreement.

The original idea had been put forward by the Head Constable. He had circulated other boroughs with a questionnaire on the matter and found that the system was already working elsewhere. Perhaps he had foreseen the council's reluctance on the matter so at the same meeting it was resolved to purchase six maroons as an experiment, these to be fired off when the men were to be called out. This was the system used by the Bromley force and the drawback is obvious - bells might awaken firemen and their families at night time but maroons would awaken the whole town. In the event the records are silent as to the results of the Reigate Borough experiment, or even as to whether it actually took place.

Tenders for a bell call-out system were sought and received from local firm Townsend, Tamplin and Makovski, from the Single Wire Telephone Company and others. All these were to be of no avail, the reason being that the full council did not seem, at this time at least, to share the Watch Committee's enthusiasm on the matter, and referred it back.

As is too often the case, events of a contentious nature have to occur before certain procedures are approved and the money spent. There were two such events, the first by far the worst yet still not quite triggering the provision of bells. This was the aforementioned 1901 fire at Nicol's of Redhill. Two lives were lost and considerable criticism levelled at the Brigade. Bells were again called for but once again nothing was done.

The second event was a fire at Mr Smith's Studios, Redhill, also in 1901. Circumstances surrounding this fire were brought up in Council after a Mr Sanders reported that he had raised the alarm by going in person to the police station. To his amazement the police had insisted they had to sent a man to the site of the reported fire to verify whether the fire brigade was needed. Only then was a policeman sent to call each of the Redhill fireman. Mr Sanders thought that this delay was unnecessary but was told that this was the rule. He said in Council that the system needed review and that electric bells were needed to summon members of the fire brigade. The Mayor remarked that his own report on the fire appliances (presumably including the use of bells) had been before that Watch Committee for four months but that no action had so far been taken. It was added that it was now understood that early action would be taken. [2]

Despite this assurance there is no mention of the matter in Watch Committee minutes until September 1902, when a single entry states: *'Firemen's houses to be connected to two stations by electric bells.'* Tenders still had to be sought and it was not until the December that Stuart and Moore's tender was accepted at £14 for one year with an option for a further seven or fourteen year contract. It would seem safe to assume that the bells would have been working some time within the first few months of 1903.

Bells were also fitted at the stables, for it was no good the fireman arriving at their station sooner if the horses took just as long as before. Whether the stable bells were indeed fitted at exactly the same time is not certain, but looking at the subject logically (often a mistake) one would expect this to be the case.

Incidentally, the house bells were reported by ex-fireman C.A.Willet, who saw service in the Reigate Brigade before the First World War, to have been so loud that not only was the whole house awoken but neighbours were roused too. It seems that great tolerance was required when there was a fireman in the road in those days.

What voltage these bells worked at, or what the source power supply was, is unknown. Electric light was supplied to the police station at Redhill in 1904 at a cost of £20.

1912 - Call-out by Bugle

Before leaving the subject of firemen's call-out completely, it ought to be recorded that there was another method, not previously mentioned, of summoning a fire fighting team, and that was by bugle call. This method was employed at the Philanthropic Farm School at Redhill where the boys manned the manual engine bought from the Reigate Corporation. Not only was there plenty of muscle power to hand but the concentration of the boys and staff at the school, although dispersed in a number of purpose-built houses, lent itself to this method of alert. The total number of fires 'alerted' in this way is unknown but there were at least two occasions.

The first was when an old pupil set fire to a haystack in 1911. He was caught and received a year's prison for the first offence but this was clearly not deterrent enough to quell the grudge he harboured against the school for he returned a second time after his release in 1912 to set fire to two more stacks, an act for which this time he received jail with hard labour. Both times the bugle called out the manual engine and the boys attacked the fires with gusto, also lending a hand on the Redhill engine when it arrived.

1902-1903 - Long Service Awards

At the beginning of the 20th century there was no system of recognising long service, a situation that prompted Fred Legg to again write a letter.

To His Worship the Mayor   *March 29th 1902*
Gentlemen of the Town Council
Application for Long Service Medal
Gentlemen
*   We beg to apply, asking you to adopt the system of presenting long service medals to members of the Borough Fire Brigades. At present we have no system of reward for long and meritorious service such as exists in many towns. We feel that we deserve some recognition for the long service which some of us have done in the Brigades, and we think that by presenting long service medals after, say, 10 years serv-*

ice, it would be an inducement to trainee members to remain in the Brigades, and would be something for the younger members to look forward to. Medals for long service have recently been presented by Chertsey, Ilford and Richmond, Battle, Selly Oak and other councils, in most cases for 10 years service with good conduct. A medal is also presented in the Metropolitan Brigade after 15 years service.

We therefore ask you, gentlemen, to give this application your favourable consideration.

Yours Respectfully.

F.Legg, J.Mason, Captains.

As a result it was decided at the Watch Committee meeting of 14th April that bronze medals would be issued for 10 years service and silver ones for 15 years. Fred Legg subsequently sent in a list of those qualifying for awards.

F.Legg	Captain	16 years 1 month
M.Crust	Foreman	31 years
E.Legg	Engineer	40 years
C.Wood	Sub-engnr	15 years 2 months
M.Whitmore		12 years
W.Wood		11 years
W.Powell		11 years

He also suggested that a bar be presented for every five years beyond the 15-year medal, and supplied a sketch of a suggested design.

In 1910 there was an article in one of the local papers detailing further long service awards. Previous to the Oddfellows centenary celebration procession the Reigate Borough firemen were drawn up outside the Municipal Buildings under command of their Chief Officer, Captain Rouse (more about him later in this chapter), and were presented with medals by the Mayoress, Mrs Gregory. Those in receipt of awards were:

F.Legg	Supt.	20 years Silver medal
J.Mason	Supt.	30 years Silver medal and two bars
W.Hockett	Foreman	35 years Silver medal and three bars
C.Wood	Foreman	20 years Silver medal
A.Whitmore	Engineer	10 years Bronze medal
T.Finch	Sub-engr	10 years Bronze medal
W.Dean	Stn Officer	15 years Bronze medal and one bar
F.Smith	Ex-fireman	10 years Bronze medal
F.Makrell	Ex-fireman	10 years Bronze medal
P.Prince	Ex-fireman	10 years Bronze medal

The above raises certain questions. The Watch Committee's decision to issue bronze medals after 10 years seems to have stood but what about the silver medal after 15 years? F.Legg should have received it in 1902 but did not in fact get it until 1910, and then for 20 years, so it looks as though the sliver medal award had been changed from 15 to 20 years, a fact borne out by Station Officer Dean getting a bronze medal and bar for 15 years.

The National Fire Brigades Union also presented long service medals, and recipients of those at a ceremony at the Municipal buildings in or around 1911 or 12 were:

M.E.Whitmore	Foreman	20 years
J.Green	Foreman	10 years
W.Wood	Engineer	20 years
W.G.Powell	Sub-engr	20 years

It has to be assumed that the above would have received long service medals from the Borough of Reigate at ceremonies for which reports have not been found during current research.

At the same ceremony the long service medal was presented by another body, the Association of Professional Fire Officers, as follows: -

| W.Dean | Stn Officer | 15 years |

Long service and good conduct certificate awarded to Brigade members, designed by Fred Legg

There was another recognition of long service, and that was the appointment of the title of 'Honorary Fireman' on long serving members at their retirement. This was conferred upon two members in 1903, M.Crust and Edwin Legg. The latter had served 47 years, being just appointed when the current manual engine had been bought. These two men were allowed to retain their uniforms, and perhaps certain privileges at Fire Brigade public events.

Reigate's horse drawn manual engine outside the station

1902-1912 - Early 1900s Incidents

The annual number of incidents was not high in the first decades of the 20th century. In 1902 there were just twelve reports of fires, the Brigades being called to only five of them, the rest being dealt with by police and public.

Records which exist for these years were as follows:

	Reports	Calls	Outside Borough
1902	12	5	not stated
1903	11	7	not stated
1904	8	6	2
1905	12	8	3
1906	16	9	3
1907	11	11	3
1908	18	14	5
1909	18	15	2
1910	15	6	2
1911	39*	27	not stated
1912	16	9	2

*(*including 11 chimney and 9 heath fires)*

Further Requests

It was May 1906 when Fred Legg asked the Council to approve the supply of a lamp showing red to be fixed to the rear of the fire engine to comply with a new bylaw. This request was approved but another made at the same time was not. This second request was for two blankets to be supplied to cover the horses, which had to stand for a long time at the site of a fire after galloping there from the station. They had to wait to pull the engine back in all weathers and at all times of year, but still the request was denied. It is said that the dog is man's best friend, but the maxim would seem not to be applicable to horses.

1908-1909 - Reigate and Redhill Brigades United Under a New Chief Officer

If the provision of a new fire station and bells for calling men out represented change then it was only a few years later when an even greater change was made. In 1908 the Council decided that the Borough would be better served if the two separate Brigades were one, and duly amalgamated them under the leadership of Chief Officer Major G.C.M.Rouse as the Reigate Borough Fire Brigade. This meant that the two existing Captains, Fred Legg at Reigate and John Mason at Redhill, had to become Superintendents under the new Chief Officer. According to Fred Legg's history this caused no friction (see appendix 2 for details of the Legg family). The HQ of the new unitary brigade was at Reigate. Although the decision was made in 1908 the amalgamation occurred in 1909, precisely one hundred years after the formation of the original Reigate Fire Service. [3]

Captain (later Major) Rouse, appointed Chief Officer of the Brigade 1909

Horse drawn wheeled escape ladder

The fact that at times there had been division and rivalry between the two towns of Redhill and Reigate has been mentioned before. That there was anything similar between the Fire Brigades of those towns, separate as two units since 1865, is unsupported by any direct evidence found during research. Nevertheless, the Reigate Watch Committee must have had sufficient reason to consider that the merger and the cost of the additional post of Chief Officer was worth the expense. They had considered other options, one of which was that Chief Constable Beacher should take the Fire Brigade under his wing. This was referred back to the Watch Committee by the Town Council, probably because it was felt that not only did Mr Beacher already have his hands full with his present duties of running the Borough Police Force but that he lacked the necessary expertise.

The Watch Committee decided to approach Captain Gerald Rouse of Blanford Road, Reigate (later of 'Lench', Blackborough Road, Reigate) regarding this new supervisory post. The rank of Captain in his case was a military one, as he had seen 15 years service in the King's Own Yorkshire Infantry. His fire fighting experience began when he served as a Metropolitan Brigade Volunteer from 1885-1888. In 1889 he founded and organised the East Worthing Fire Brigade, in which he served as Chief Officer. He was subsequently requested by Worthing Council to draw up a scheme for a Borough Fire Brigade when its Charter of Incorporation was obtained in 1892, which he did. His scheme was adopted and he served as second officer for a while.

Above: Redhill's horse drawn manual, Hospital Fund parade 1905
Below: Redhill firemen outside the Police station, with their manual engine & competition trophies

Captain Fred Legg with Reigate Brigade members outside their new station in Castle field Road, with some of their equipment, including a hand cart

Above: Reigate compete at Guildford cattle market in a hose cart competition
Below: Reigate hose cart winners

It was in May 1909, that the Watch Committee decided to offer Captain Rouse the job. On 1st July, at Firlands, Reigate Road, the premises of Surgeon General Robert Rouse, police extinguished a rubbish fire. The alarm was raised by Captain Rouse who was about to become Chief Officer of the Borough Brigades.

An early public duty for Captain Rouse after his appointment was at the Fire Brigade Competition held at the Headquarters Station, Castlefield Road, Reigate, in early September 1909. Four Redhill men had taken part. Captain Rouse made a speech at the official dinner that evening and some of his comments reflected on the subject of his appointment and the results achieved thus far. What he said raises one or two questions about the possibility that not all might have been quite as harmonious as it might have been between the two Brigades. The newspaper reported him as saying:

'All of those present know how the circumstances arose by which I have come into this Brigade, and I would like to take this opportunity of saying how greatly I appreciate the good feeling and good comradeship which has been extended to me by the officers and men. When I speak of the Brigade I do not speak of it as it has been described in the press and by the public, as being two separate and distinct bodies; ours is a Borough Brigade, (hear, hear) but a line has been drawn between Reigate and Redhill. I have been appointed Chief Officer and, as you are aware, the Brigade has been divided into two districts, of which Reigate is 'A' district and Redhill is 'B' district. We are only too pleased this year to receive the officers and men of 'B' district as our guests but hope that in future this function will be a 'Brigade' show (hear, hear).

'I would like to express my appreciation of the way in which the officers and men have worked under me. From the time I first consulted Superintendents Legg and Mason as for the ideas for the conduct of the Brigade I have felt that I could not have better officers (applause). I wish tonight to strike a note of unity. A house divided against itself could not stand, and the same observation applied to the Fire Brigade, for we can only find success by acting as one body. The success of our Brigade depends upon the units of which it is composed: if they all work together with their officers the result will be success, but if schism is introduced it will only mean one thing, and that is failure. That would reflect discredit on you all. As you are now constituted you have the makings of a fine corps, and I ask that in the future we work together, shoulder to shoulder, for the good of your Brigade (applause).'

This speech reinforces conjecture about the independence of the two, previously separate, Brigades of Redhill and Reigate, but says much more, being full of phrases such as *'a line drawn between'*, *'a house divided against itself'* and *'if schism is introduced'*. These imply a split but of themselves make far less impact than the fact that the majority of the officers and men of the Redhill Brigade were not present at the evening function. The exception to this was Superintendent J.Mason, who was present as a visitor.

After more than 53 years of independence it is no real surprise that the two Brigades had gone their own ways. Each Brigade held its own events, but whether Redhill had competitions is uncertain, for Supt. Mason, in his speech, said that there was a lack of opportunity for good drill at the Redhill end of the Borough, a fault that would be remedied if the two districts worked together. This observation probably was a reference to the fact that compared with Reigate, Redhill lacked facilities at its station, which was probably little more than a storeroom for the engine and appliances. Back in 1903 Captain Mason had arranged for occasional drills to be carried out at the Redhill and Reigate Hospital in Whitepost Hill. Incidentally, the timing of the Reigate Brigade's 4th of September, 1909, event was good in bringing the men to peak condition, for only a few days later, on Wednesday the 8th, there was another competition held in conjunction with the Reigate Carnival. This time there was evidence of a split between the two towns (not the Brigades) as it had been suggested that this

Reigate and Redhill full turn out c1921

Bell Challenge Shield, ambulance competition winners

be Reigate's carnival, not anyone else's, and it was very late in the day when this idea was given up and Redhill Town was allowed to have some share in the proceedings. Indeed, this was the Fire Brigade's first ever part in the Reigate carnival, and the Reigate Brigade arranged a competion at the Sports Ground in London Road under the auspices of the National Fire Brigade's Union, restricted to brigades within Surrey, with proceeds going towards the Provincial Police orphanage in Redhill. A number of other brigades took part, with the Metropolitan Water Board's Brigade being the most successful prize taker. Reigate's only success was in the escape competition when its team saw off the rest with a far superior time and won the Colman Shield. Once again it seems that Redhill Brigade was not represented.

There was another reason for certain inactivity from the Redhill Brigade. In this year of 1909 it had already been noted in the local press that not only had it not joined in with any of the local parades but it had not held a parade of its own that in previous years had collected money for the local hospital on Whitepost Hill. This was because in past years some towns had joined in parades to raise money for county funds while others did not. In view of this 'some do and some don't' situation, Redhill's contention was that one Sunday should be set aside for county parades in all towns, county charities benefiting as a result, and until that happened it was unfair for Surrey to expect some towns to contribute whilst some did not. No parade at all in 1909 was Redhill's way of giving this matter a higher profile.

The trouble with this attitude was that the local hospital fund suffered, whilst criticism was directed at Redhill by some observers, coupled with a feeling that they ought to join in with Reigate in this matter.

Exchange visit with Horley Fire Brigade

This was perhaps a syndrome of the Redhill/Reigate 'them and us' situation but maybe it politicised the situation of their separateness to the point where amalgamation of the Fire Brigades was seen as the right and proper thing to do. While we can only speculate about the feelings of the individual members of the two forces on the merger, other than the slight evidence in the phrases used in the speech of Chief Officer Rouse there is nothing to suggest that the amalgamation of the two Brigades was anything but amicable.

More About Parades
Parades were a way of life for firemen who were part of the Borough force. They were present at a number of annual events each year in different parts of the Borough where scouts bearing banners, friendly societies, ambulance services, Church Lads Brigades and the town band joining together must have made a very large contingent. Monies collected were usually for a couple of local charities, one of which was, as stated, often connected with the Redhill and Reigate Hospital.

As well as the celebratory parades, where money was collected for good causes and people generally had a good time, there were the more solemn occasions. These included the Mayoral church service, held at least once a year; funerals, such as that of King Edward Vll in 1910; Coronations; Jubilees, such as that of Queen Victoria in 1897; and visits by royalty, such as those of Princess Christian to the Police Orphanage in 1904 and of the Duchess of Albany to the same establishment in 1911. To many of these events the presence of members of one of the Fire Brigades with an

*Above: **Reigate Brigade parade through Town Centre***
*Below: **Royal National Life Boat parade***

engine was always a crowd-puller. Unsurprisingly, therefore, there were a number of times when the presence of an engine was requested by an event organiser, or even its loan or hire was requested. These were always refused; either the Brigade was there in an official capacity, with the engine, or there was no fire presence at all. When the Brigade was to be present then it had to have the permission of the Watch Committee.

Finance

The charge for the hire of horses over the years had no doubt slowly increased with inflation and also varied according to whether their use was for a fire or for a drill. By 1909 the rate for a pair of horses for use at a fire was 2 guineas, and for each extra horses 1 guinea. Horses supplied for drills cost less at 15/- each. The coachman's rate was 5/- per fire and 1/- per drill. These rates were specified separately for A and B districts, and although they were identical amounts for each after 1909 they may have been different in previous years.

No doubt these arrangements were well entrenched in local business practices after a century of practical application. They would have needed to be from the very beginning as the last thing anyone would have wanted was for the stable to be alerted, the horses readied, the fireman waiting for the off, and then for there to have been wrangling over payment. It is assumed, possibly rashly, that horses were supplied without question and payment made within due course. No doubt there were hiccoughs, but for such essential and serious work the most difficult part was probably the shaking into wakefulness of the stableman and the convincing of the horses, especially at night, that they really did have to leave the peace and quiet of their warm, hay-strewn quarters and go out, often into the cold and rain, to work for their living.

Payment being made 'in due course' might have meant that there were times when the vendor had to wait for his money and times when he had to prompt the council for payment. A letter to the Watch Committee from Sam Marsh, Redhill stable owner, in 1892, resulted in a payment to him of £6.7.6, no small amount in those days, and was, perhaps, an example of one of those times.

Wrangling over payment would not have achieved a great deal in 1909 for two reasons. One was that the rates were already well established, the other was that all sums over £1 had to be sanctioned by the Watch Committee. The Chief Officer could sanction payments under this figure.

These costs were recouped, at least in some degree, by the Council via charges levied upon those who received the services of the Fire Brigade. For the attendance of an engine at a fire the charge was 3 guineas plus the cost of conveyance to and from the fire. Also the owner of the attended premises was liable for all the attending firemen's pay and any damage to their uniforms or equipment. Clearly a fire could well be a very expensive event for the unfortunate owner of the premises. Not only would he have fire and water damage, which he was at liberty to decide how and when to rectify according to his circumstances, but he would receive, probably within the month, a fairly substantial bill that would not carry so much choice.

The general costs of the Borough Brigade, like most other costs, would have risen steadily over the years. Brigade pay stood at £27 for the year in 1892. It was paid half yearly, whether in advance or arrears is unknown but probably the latter. The actual structure of payments at this time is uncertain; it is known that the Captains (and later the resident fireman) received regular pay (or retainers) and that expenses, or call-out money, was paid additionally to all ranks. In a subsequent part of this history these retainers and expenses are detailed. In January 1902, the Captains' pay rose to £1.5s per quarter.

A note in Fred Legg's report book states that the total pay of the Brigade was increased to £4-17-6 quarterly from December 25th 1897. There is no mention of this in the Watch Committee minutes but the matter may have been dealt with purely by the Finance Committee. This does account for

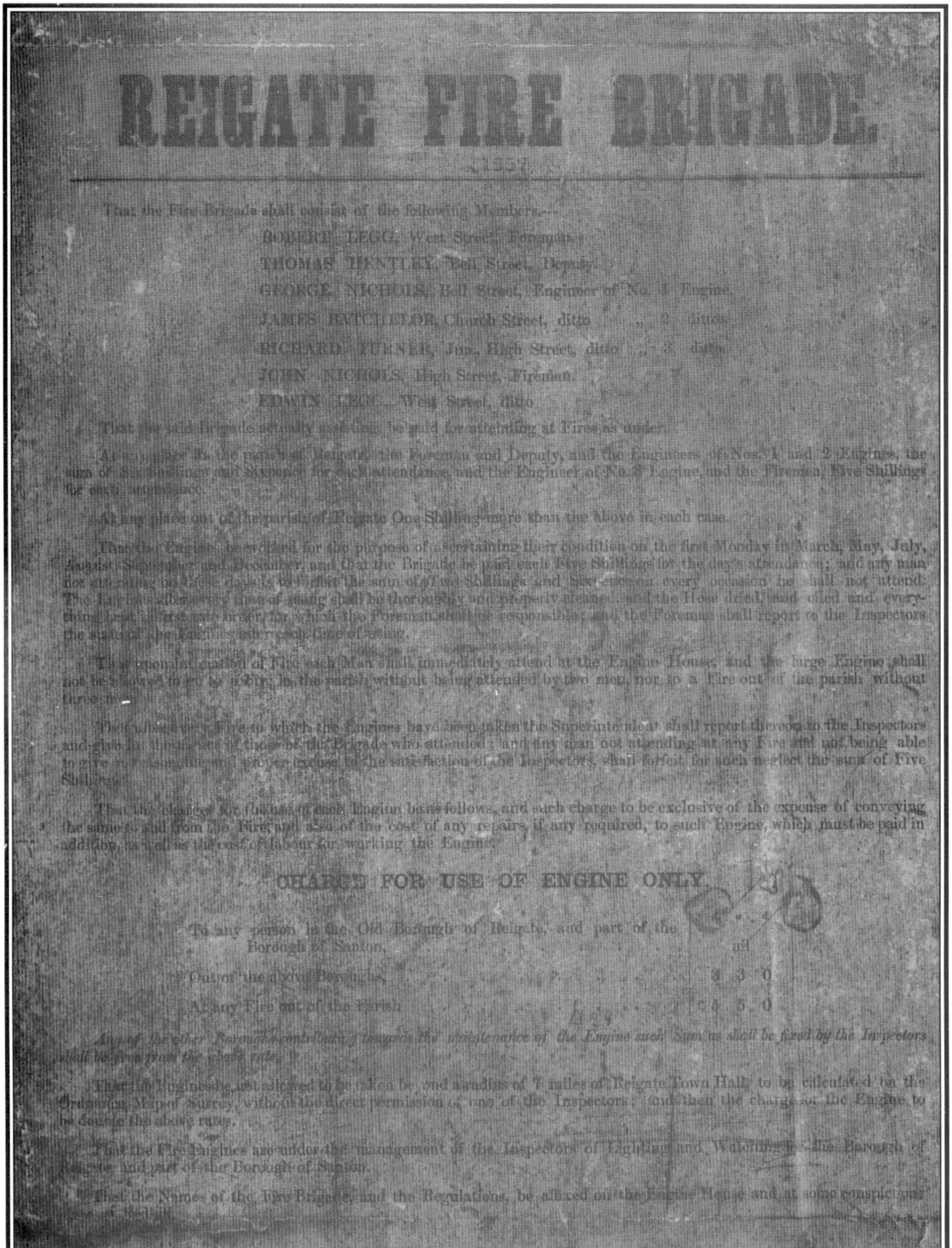

Early charge board for the use of the engine

the annual pay bill rising to £39 by 1899, and another increase must have raised it further for it stood at £49 in 1903. Expenses were paid for attendance at fires at fixed rates, for subsequent engine and hose cleaning and drying, and there were payments for additional duties such as drills.

1897 was a good year for the Borough Police Force as it was Queen Victoria's Jubilee Year and each member received two days extra pay, probably for additional duties rather than in commemoration of the event. There was no mention of a similar payment to members of the Borough Fire Brigade.

The Fire Brigade was by far the less expensive of the two Borough services. A breakdown of Fire Brigade costs looked like this: -

Pay	£93
Horses hire for drills	£6
Sub-Station rents	£11
Maintenance of electric bells	£20
Fuel and light	£29
Expenses at fires	£100
Hydrants	£30
Hose	£30
Chemical extinguishers	£8
Ladders and gear	£11
Repairing engines	£8
Respirators, gloves and medals	£10
Life lines, straps and belts	£10
Uniforms, boots etc.	£20
Harness and appliances	£21
Cleaning materials	£7
Sundries	£22
Rates, tax and Insurance	£15
Printing, Stationery and petty	£10
Telephones	£14
TOTAL	**£475**

Although there is no major equipment expenditure in the above list, as there might have been if ladders had been purchased or extensive engine repairs had been made or new engines bought, the annual outlay would still not have approached that of £4,172 for the police.

Pay and allowances were as follows, being taken from the Borough of Reigate Rules and Regulations and Scale of Pay and Charges and Outline of Duties for 1909.

Rank	*Call Money*	*After 1st three hrs*
Chief Officer	——	——
Superintendent	8/6	2/6 per hour
Foreman	7/6	2/- " "
Engineer	7/-	2/- " "
Sub-engineer	6/6	1/6 " "
Firemen	6/-	1/- " "
Reserve men		1/- " "
Pay to be reckoned from time of call		

Outside the Borough the Chief Officer will be paid 21/- for attendance

<u>*Chimney Fires.*</u> *Half the above rate of call money when no appliances other than sulphur are used. Where appliances or ladders are used the usual rates of pay.*

<u>*Chief Officer's Allowance.*</u> *The C.O. will receive the sum of £12.12.0 per annum, payable quarterly, for uniform and personal expenses.*

<u>*Superintendent's Allowance.*</u> *Superintendents will receive the sum of £5 per annum, payable quarterly.*

<u>*Foreman's Allowance.*</u> *Foremen will receive the sum of £5 per annum, payable quarterly.*

All Members below the rank of Foreman will receive 30/- per annum, payable quarterly. These payments to include drills and test alarms.

<u>*Cleaning Allowance After Fires.*</u>	*£ s d*
For cleaning fire engine or horsed escape	*2 0 0*
" " hose cart and complement	
(not exceeding 600 ft of hose)	*1 0 0*
If more than 600 ft of hose is used £1 0 0 extra	
the whole not to exceed	*2 0 0*

<u>*Horse Hire for Fires*</u> *The Chief Officer shall have the power to order horses when necessary for attendance at fires. Horse hire shall be paid as under:-*

Within the Borough Area

A District	*Pair of horses*	*Two guineas*
B District	*" "*	*Two guineas*
	Extra horses (if required)	*One guinea*

Outside the Borough Area

A District	*Pair of horses*	*Three guineas*
B District	*" "*	*Three guineas*
	Extra horses (if required)	*One guinea*

<u>*Coachman's Pay.*</u> *Such sums to be exclusive of the coachman's money, who shall receive the sum of 5/- for fires and 1/- for drills*

<u>*Horse Hire for Drills.*</u> *The Chief Officer may order horses for drill purposes. Such drills not to exceed 4 for each district in 12 months. Horse hire shall be paid for as under:-*

A District	*Fifteen shillings*
B District	*Fifteen shillings*

1910-1911 - Obsolete and Useless Equipment

Victims of fire were not the only ones with large bills as Borough ratepayers were faced with the task of financing substantial expenditure in 1910 in order to bring the Brigade's equipment up-to-date. It was the appointment of Chief Officer Rouse which brought about this capital expenditure. A new broom sweeps clean and Captain Rouse was endeavouring to get the Reigate force properly equipped. In order to achieve this he had recommended extra fire telephones be fitted around the towns and had condemned the current escape ladder as useless. This history has previously recorded the 1901 rejection by the Horley Captain of Reigate Town Council's attempt to get rid of an outdated and apparently unsellable-elsewhere escape ladder. Was this the same one? It seems likely that it was either the same one, or at least one of similar age, for accounts of the deliberations regarding a replacement record Councillor H.Ongley saying that since he had been in the Borough he could not recall the ladder being used. Exactly how long the Councillor had been in the Borough is unknown, but he had been Mayor for two years from 1895-7, was a Reigate tradesman, and so most probably went back much further than that. Certainly 1901 falls within his experience. This meant that by 1910 the escape was probably twenty years old at least, bearing out another remark made at the time about it to the effect that because it had been good enough for grandfather did not mean that it was still good enough. Two escape ladders had been bought from Shand Mason by the Council in 1890, so the ladder in question could have been one of these. All references seem to be in the singular, however, so the question raised is what became of the other one? If the ladder is not one of these but an even older one there would still - at least at one time - have been a pair due to the earlier policy of keeping the two Brigades (when they were separate entities) similarly equipped, although the years could well have seen the demise of one of such a pair of even more ancient ladders.

The result of the 1910 deliberations concerning equipment upgrades and extra fire telephones was mixed. Some concern was felt at the cost and effectiveness of the telephonic fire points and they were referred back to the Watch Committee - not technically a vote against its recommendation by full Council but a signal for it to reconsider its proposal. The purchase of a new horsed escape and tender from Bayleys Ltd. at £140, was another item approved by the Watch Committee which was only to be referred back by the Council. It was suggested by one Councillor that it might be better to get a motorised escape but this idea was also rejected.

Later that year there was a rather confusing recommendation that a horsed escape and tender be purchased for £200, £60 more than the original tender, but whatever kind of a red herring this might have been the original purchase finally gained full approval and the item was bought at £140. It was duly supplied and in January of 1911 Chief Officer Rouse was giving his report on it to the Council.

Another suggestion, that hanging harnesses should be obtained was also rejected. (These were harnesses hung so that horses could walk into them, designed as a time saver). The money required for the horsed escape was to be borrowed by the Council. In addition, plans submitted by Captain Rouse for a new sub-station to be built at South Park were approved.

The success of these representations for renewal and modernisation were due in no little part to the esteem with which Captain Rouse seemed to be held, but a Councillor is said to have revealed that Captain Rouse had threatened to resign if his requests were not met. This seems a little improbable at this early point in the service of the new Chief Officer as the Council responsible for his appointment would be unlikely to not support his recommendations and thereby be seen to not be backing their choice. Perhaps this is what the Captain was banking on, choosing to strike hard and early in order to get what he wanted. Perhaps he had his detractors within the Council but was sure enough of his supporters to obtain overall backing.

Having said that, it does seem that he was admired in Council. He was also admired and backed by the local press, the fact that he had served in London under Captain Shaw, a very famous officer of the previous century, counting greatly in his favour. He did not get all of his own way, however, and perhaps by allowing some and refusing some the Council trod a line of compromise which was acceptable to the Captain. An example of this came the following year when Captain Rouse's recommendation that the firemen of Earlswood and South Park had call bells and that their stations be linked with other sections of the Redhill and Reigate Brigade was turned down. Once again the press were on Captain Rouse's side, likening the Council's decision to spoiling the ship for a halfpennyworth of tar. The cost would have been £36. A letter in the local paper pointed out that if a telephone was used to call a Brigade to a fire at Earlswood it would have to call the Redhill Brigade as they were connected to the service and Earlswood was not, thereby causing unnecessary delay. Shortly after this an application by the Chief Officer for new 'undress jackets' for the Brigade was also refused.

1909-1912 - The Growing Importance of the Telephone

Today the telephone and other forms of electric and electronic communication are vital tools for alerting the Fire Brigade, but at the beginning of the century this was far less the case. The first use of the telephone in the Borough appears to have been the link between the two branches of T.S.Marriage in Redhill and Reigate in April 1883. The local telephone service proper did not begin until nine years later in Redhill in 1892 and must have been of limited use at first because of the few numbers of telephones in use, and even fewer available to the public. The police were less speedy than Marriages to recognise the benefit of this new technology; it was in January of 1893 when they were discussing the telephone link between the Redhill and Reigate stations set up on a trial basis. The trial must have been a success because they continued its use, paying £12.13.9 per annum for the service.

The Fire Brigade had also realised the benefits of the new facility. It was run by the same Council as the police but there is no evidence to show that the two fire stations were connected by telephone at the same time as the police, although it was done within a few years.

By the end of 1909 the number of ordinary telephones in use generally had increased considerably, as had the number of dedicated fire telephones situated in the towns for the purpose of alerting the local Brigade to fires. There were four such telephones in the area, with another six said to be required. In February 1910, nine or ten more telephones were proposed to be provided at South Park, Frenches Corner, Shaw's Corner, Croydon Road, Meadvale, Earlswood, near the New Inn on the Brighton Road, and at St Mary's Road, Reigate. There were those on the Council who queried the cost of this provision and asked what the return would be. They were told that they should forget monetary return, and that if one life was saved through their use then that was ample return enough. Those doubters persevered, nevertheless, convincing the main body of opinion that at a rate of 132 fires in 10 years, many in haystacks and chimneys and the like, it was unlikely they would be of practical benefit, merely providing fun for mischievous boys. The request was eventually referred back to the Watch Committee.

Whether or not life was ever directly saved by use of the existing fire points is unknown, nor is how long they remained available for use. What is known from published statistics is that of the sixteen fires in 1912, three were reported by the public telephone service and two by police telephones, there being no mention of the fire alarm telephones. Telephonic reports of fires were still a minority, however, as information about seven others were conveyed to the Fire Brigade by messenger. Like many other innovations, the telephone needed time to become familiar enough to the public for the instrument to be freely used with comfort and confidence.

1911 - Technology and Reigate Hill

If the emerging importance of electricity was a sign of the times then another such sign of the times was that one of the fires of 1911 was caused by the fusing of electric wires. This showed that there were old hazards springing from new sources, some of which would require new techniques to deal with them. Electrical fires would become more and more common and would require an understanding of their special problems.

Another one of the new sources of fires was the motor car. With highly inflammable liquids being used in their power generation it was not surprising that fires occurred, but it was not always the engines or their fuel that was the source of the problem. Reigate had a geographical hazard in Reigate Hill. During descent vehicles relied heavily on their brakes, and overheating during the long descent could start body fires that resulted in the total destruction of the vehicle, as happened in 1911 to an open taxi - a landaulette of the Unic Taxi-cab Company of London - travelling from London to Brighton.

The same year there was another Reigate Hill vehicle fire, this time involving a pantechnicon travelling north at 1.45 in the morning. The vehicle consisted of two furniture-laden trailers being pulled by a steam tractor. A coupling broke and the rear trailer ran back down the hill, colliding with a lamppost. The impact broke an oil lamp on the rear trailer, the oil igniting and setting light to the trailer. Much of the furniture belonging to the ex-manager of the London and Counties Bank in Reigate, who was removing to a London location, was destroyed.

These are just two examples of countless fires to vehicles that have occurred locally since, but due to modern safety standards and technological advance, Reigate Hill ceases to be the hazard it once was.

1909-1913 - Competition

This history contains dry statistics which might make it seem that the stuff of the every day existence of a suburban fire force consisted mainly of such things. In 1912 the Reigate Borough Fire Brigade consisted of (more statistics): 1 Chief Officer, 2 Superintendents, 3 Foreman, 2 Engineers, 1 Station Officer, 2 Sub Officers, 25 Firemen, 5 Reserve men and 3 Coachmen, making 44 men in all. What else, apart from fighting fires, drilling frequently to hone their equipment familiarity and expertise, cleaning their equipment and generally waiting for fires to happen was there for them to do? The answer was for the best of them to take part in competitions to demonstrate and display their art (if that is the right word) and their general level of competence.

These competitions were held at local as well as at county level. Cups and shields were on offer, to be proudly display at home stations, for various standard drills and performances under timed competition conditions. In his 1912 report to the Watch Committee, Major Rouse was able to report that Reigate Borough Brigade men had won the Boulton Challenge Cup for a 4-man drill at the Surrey District competition. The winning crew consisted of Station Officer Dean, firemen R.Woodhouse, G.Tickner and A.Woodhouse. The winner of the Inglis Challenge Shield for the best 1-man manual drill was Fireman G.Hockett from Reigate B District with an aggregate time of just under 214 seconds. This was a time he bettered in 1913, winning again in 198 seconds. The Reigate District Shield was won by B Division, the winning crew being Engineer A.Whitmore, Fireman C.Winchester, G.Hockett and E.Easton. These were just some of the results of competitions for that year.

Such activities had been going on for many years. The Fire Brigade's Association of Surrey had been formed in 1862 and it became the Surrey branch of the National Fire Brigade's Union in 1887. At various times Challenge Trophies had been presented to be competed for annually in Surrey. The County competition, or tournament as it was often called, was held in various towns, attract-

Pump competition winners, 1930s

ing the public and its money, which usually went towards some good cause locally, often the local Hospital Saturday Fund and the Widows and Orphans Fund of the Fire Brigades Union.

In some towns it was said that the fire brigade was considered a necessary evil, and that its members were ranked with dustmen and sanitary men. Worse, it was also felt that the public had an idea that there was nothing to learn in fire fighting and (probably even worse still) that anyone could be a successful Chief Officer. Whether or not this public image of the service was indeed truly held, annual competitions were seen by those in command as educating the public away from any kind of misconception and improving their perception of a fire fighting force whose job was to save their property and their lives. Not only that, but in the absence of fires it was necessary to keep the various brigades efficient and always alert. Competition honed skills to perfection, gave added purpose and direction to what must have sometimes been less than riveting drill procedures, created personal and local pride in the acquired professional skills of its servants and, not least, enlivened the whole of the host town for a day.

The local equivalent of the Surrey tournaments was the annual drills. These appear not to have had such a long pedigree, for the fourth of these to be organised by the Reigate District force was held in 1909 at the parade ground of the Municipal Buildings, Reigate. The competition judges were Captain Whaley of the Dorking Fire Brigade and ex-Foreman Crust of the Borough Fire Brigade. Various drills were performed against the clock, including a demonstration of a Bayley Curricle fire escape by Supt. F.Legg, who succeeded in wheeling it out, extending it and putting it into operation in 171.5 seconds. [4] The newspaper report stated that there was considerable public interest in the event; clearly there was media interest as 21 inches of Surrey Mirror column space was devoted to the report of the day, including details of the competitions and their results as well as of the speeches given at the dinner that followed in the evening.

The 1913 competition was held at a new venue, the grounds of Reigate Lodge, which had then been acquired by the Corporation.

Castlefield Road drill tower being used with gas flood lighting

Above and below: Brigade display fire fighting techniques at Reigate Lodge.

Speeches and awards following the Brigade display at Reigate Lodge.

Reigate Borough competitions were supplemented by a series of challenges between three services of the Borough, the Fire Brigade, the Police and the Postmen. The first of these took place in the Reigate Priory in 1911. Admission was free but it was envisaged that future events would raise money for charity through an entrance fee. The day's competition resulted in a clean sweep for the police. They won the tug-of-war, the relay race and the throwing the cricket ball. Other events were more in the novelty vein and involved races wherein uniforms had to be swapped with other competitors, resulting in various situations of ludicrously over or undersized garments, including helmets, being worn. Humour, it was emphasised in the newspaper article reporting the event, was a sign of the good feeling that existed between the three services.

More about 1912
The manual engines were only used on four occasions this year as two fires were dealt with by chemical extinguishers, one by use of a hand pump and three with buckets. Three more fires were extinguished by use of hydrants of which, by this time, there were one hundred and eighty-four in the Borough. Scaling ladders were used five times and Pompier ladders once. [5] Almost six and a half thousand feet of hose was used in total and the amount of fire damage was assessed at £1,345. As £24,897 worth of property was considered to be risked then we might calculate that £23,552 worth of property was saved by Fire Brigade attendances.

Purchased in 1912:
> 1000 ft of 2 ¾ inch canvas, with couplings and straps
> 200ft 1 ¾ inch hose
> 1 water tower nozzle
> 1 double swivel headed standpipe

4 pairs of round threaded couplings
5 electric handlamps
6 hose clamps
1 pole ladder
4 folding Pompier ladders
120ft 2 ½ inch manila rope
100ft 2 inch manila rope

1909 - Duties and Responsibilities

The following resume is based on the 1909 'Borough of Reigate Rules and Regulations, Scale of Pay and Charges and Outline of Duties'.

The Chief Officer

The Chief Officer had charge of the whole of the Reigate Borough Brigade and was directly responsible to the Watch Committee. He had the power to suspend any member of the Brigade who acted otherwise than in accordance with its strict rules and regulations.

The Superintendent

Each of the two Superintendents had charge of a district, including the sub-districts. They carried out their duties in accordance with the directions of the Chief Officer but had direct control of the men and equipment in their district. They notified the Chief Officer of each and every fire call but then were in command of the response to that call, making the decision as to how many men and appliances should attend. One thing they had to bear in mind was that no matter how serious a fire outside the Borough might be, regulations forbade the use of both engines at that fire, one engine plus the men to work it, having to remain within the Borough at all times.

The Superintendent was also responsible for the day-to-day organisation of his Division, seeing that the duty roster and other books were properly maintained and that reports, especially those of fires, were made out and promptly supplied to the Chief Officer. After fires he was responsible for seeing that the men were organised on cleaning duties and record the hours to be paid for such extra work. He was also responsible for the discipline of the men under him.

The Foreman

The Foreman was the assistant and deputy to the Superintendent. He saw that the Superintendent's orders were carried out and, in his absence, took charge. This rank had a long history that was close to its end in the sub-districts of the Reigate/Redhill area. In 1913 in these sub-districts the rank of Foreman was abolished and the senior fireman in each was given the title of Sub-Officer in charge.

The Engineer

The Engineer in each district had charge of the maintenance of the manual fire engine and all the gear that belonged to it. How far he was able to go in effecting repairs is unclear, as some defects would have needed specialised equipment to repair, but he was, no doubt, possessed of the necessary tools and abilities to be able to keep the engine running under most normal circumstances. It was his responsibility to report all defects to his Superintendent, and should specialised attention be required, either for wood, metal or leather repairs, then presumably that expertise would be hired in.

The Sub-Engineer

This officer was responsible for the fire escape and its equipment.

Officer of the Week

The foremen, Engineers and Sub-Engineers took it in turns to visit stations to ensure that all was as it should be at each installation. They would sign the Occurrence Book to show that their visit had been made and that all Brigade rules in force were being adhered to.

One of those rules was that 'Any Member of the Brigade on Theatre or Special duty quitting his post, or smoking, shall be suspended by the visiting officer and brought before the Chief Officer, who shall report the same to the Watch Committee.' Whilst quitting one's post is clearly a very serious breach of duty, smoking, even in the context of a fire prevention occupation, seems to be a slightly surprising inclusion bearing in mind how many men smoked in days when its health hazards were unrecognised. It was almost a national pastime, and only a few years later women were sending cigarettes in their millions in the name of 'comforts' to men fighting abroad during the Great War. Those same men would write home saying how grateful they were for their 'comforts' and how they did not know how they would have managed without them. This is not to compare the awfulness of trench warfare far from home with the local war against fire, but these were in many cases the same men, or men of the same social strata, and it is wondered how many firemen were non-smokers. Abstinence from the weed would seem to have been an advantage in face of this rule.

Resident Firemen

Firemen at this time were almost all on call. One exception was the Resident Fireman. He lived in a flat that was a part of the new fire station in the Municipal Buildings with his wife and family and attended the fire station daily, signing the occurrence Book when he opened and closed the station within set hours. He was present to receive the first notification of any fire that might occur and to set in motion the necessary call-out procedures. When there was no such actions in progress he made sure that all was well, with engines and equipment, uniforms and stores, as well as the premises itself, clean, in good condition and ready for use. Although not the case at first, rules were later introduced to ensure continuation of the duties when the resident engineer was absent, the other firemen taking it in turns to cover his duty.

1902-1913 - The First Resident Fireman at Reigate's New Headquarters

There was originally some difference of opinion as to which of the Borough's two main services should supply the resident at the Municipal Buildings. Clearly the Fire Brigade thought that it should be one of their men when, in October 1901, Fred Legg recommended Sub-engineer C.T.Wood for the job. He stated that Fireman Wood was ideal by merit of being married with no family, a total abstainer and permanently employed as foreman blacksmith at Burtenshaw's carriage works.

At a meeting of the Watch Committee in February of 1902, however, it was the members' opinion that the resident man ought to be drawn from the Borough Constabulary, as the police station was also situated there. Opinion polarised when a resolution passed at its April meeting was that a married fireman be chosen to reside there. He would clean the engine and other appliances and assist the caretaker in his duties, whilst his wife would search prisoners if necessary. Also it was noted that in the Municipal Buildings were five hydrants, which were to be cleaned by the caretaker and tested by the Brigade. In June, 1902, Fireman W.H.Dean was appointed Resident Fireman at 20/- per week plus fire and light (despite a letter in which 1902 Fred Legg had suggested that the pay should be 22/- per week). The fact of the weekly wage meant that Fireman Dean was thereby permanently employed this way, Fred Legg's choice of Sub-engineer C.T.Wood not apparently being eligible by virtue of his current full employment elsewhere.

Fireman Dean, whilst accepting the post was applying for a pay rise in August of 1903, a request which was refused. Undeterred he applied again in the December and had his pay raised to 22/- per week with the inclusion of an undress uniform.

His duties were constant to the point where he was always on duty. This seems unbelievable but a letter written by Fred Legg on June 13th, 1903, pointed out to the members of the Watch Committee: *'that resident fireman W.Dean is practically always on duty. The only time he can get away is when another fireman volunteers to stay at the station while he is away. I beg to suggest...that he be permitted to have one day clear leave in each month, and that he give notice to the police of his intention of being absent on the day chosen....'* This request was granted the same month and 7/6d was allowed to cover the cost of a replacement for that day. In January 1904, following a further letter from Fred Legg, it was resolved that the caretaker would cover the Resident Fireman's duties when that man was absent. This included informing the police when an alarm of fire was given at the fire station. One day a month was not very much and his duties must have been fairly restricting, especially where his social life was concerned. Things continued to improve, however, as in September of 1906 he was given permission to be absent from duty for one evening per week, presumably in addition to the one clear day per month.

Fireman Dean did not occupy all the rooms over the fire station, as unoccupied ones were let to Fireman William Ware at 6/- per week in July of 1905. This same year the Reigate Baths were opened and required a Superintendent. The baths being opposite the Municipal Buildings presented an opportunity for Fireman Dean, an ambitious man as we shall see later, to earn extra money by filling that post. A letter was written by Fred Legg to the Watch Committee objecting to this, saying that his time at the fire station was too short already, a marked contrast to his 1903 letter asking that Fireman Dean be allowed time off. With unfortunate timing Fireman Dean injured his knee at a drill just over a month after Fred Legg's letter objecting to his doing extra duty and so, for a while at least, was unavailable for any duty. It was shortly after this, in October 1906, when Fred Legg's request to the Watch Committee to allow Fireman Dean one evening off per week was made.

The Baths Committee had to find a man from elsewhere, but having found their man had to house him. They applied in February 1907 for space over the fire station but were told there was no room. With more unfortunate timing Fireman Ware died the following month so the rooms were then offered to the Baths Committee.

That same February Fireman Dean had again applied for a wage increase but it is not recorded whether this request was granted. Another request followed in 1910 when his wage was advanced by 3/- per week but it was resolved that in future no money would be paid to him for fire attendances. In 1911 Fireman Dean was given a long service award. He had started his service in 1894 so was two years overdue for his 15 year medal. Two years later, in 1913, his application for a pay rise was again refused but within months he had resigned. His ambition seems to have been realised for he was leaving to go to Sutton Coldfield to take up the post of Chief Officer there. This seems an amazing advancement, from fireman to Chief Officer in one jump, but then he was a professional, full-time fireman, quite a rare thing it seems in those days, so would have had plenty of good experience in techniques and procedures, although presumably none of command. Presumably he also had other qualities which stood him in good stead. Although he has here been continuously referred to as Fireman Dean he is in several accounts referred to as Station Officer Dean, although no mention has been found in records of the creation of this rank close to this time. In the local press report of his resignation he is referred to again as Resident Fireman Dean, so perhaps Station Officer was an alternative title preferred by some parties - Firemen Dean himself perhaps, if he was indeed a man of ambition as seems to be the case. He was given a testimonial, awarded two guineas in lieu of uniform not provided, and his resignation was effective from August 28th. Fireman Alfred Charles

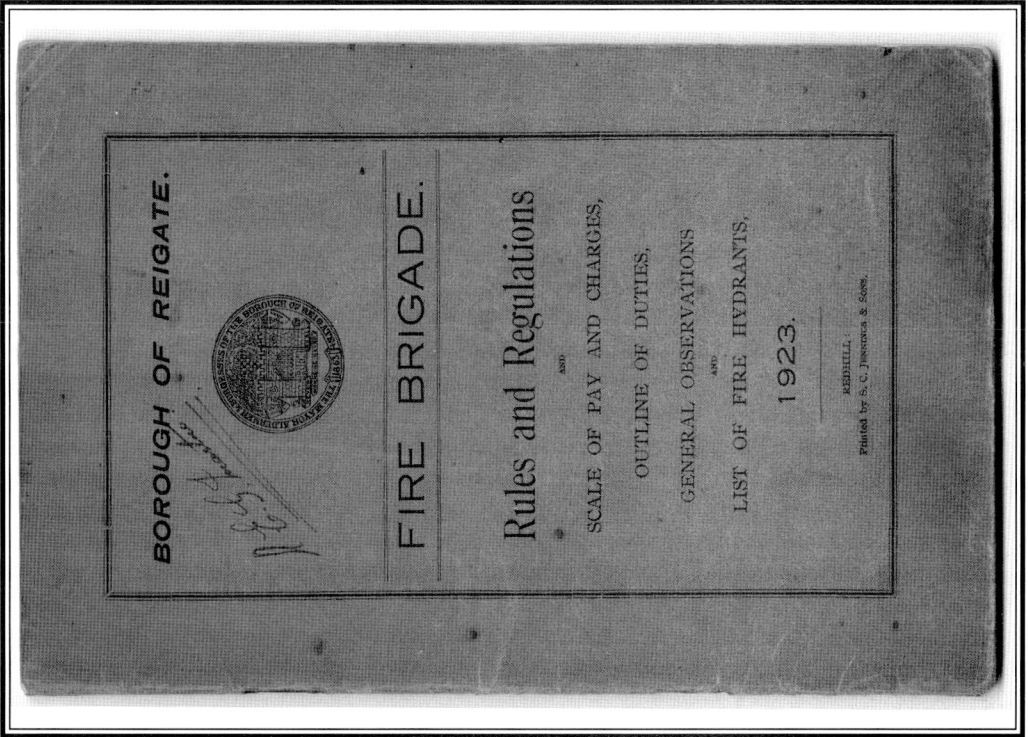

Rules and regulations of the Brigade 1923

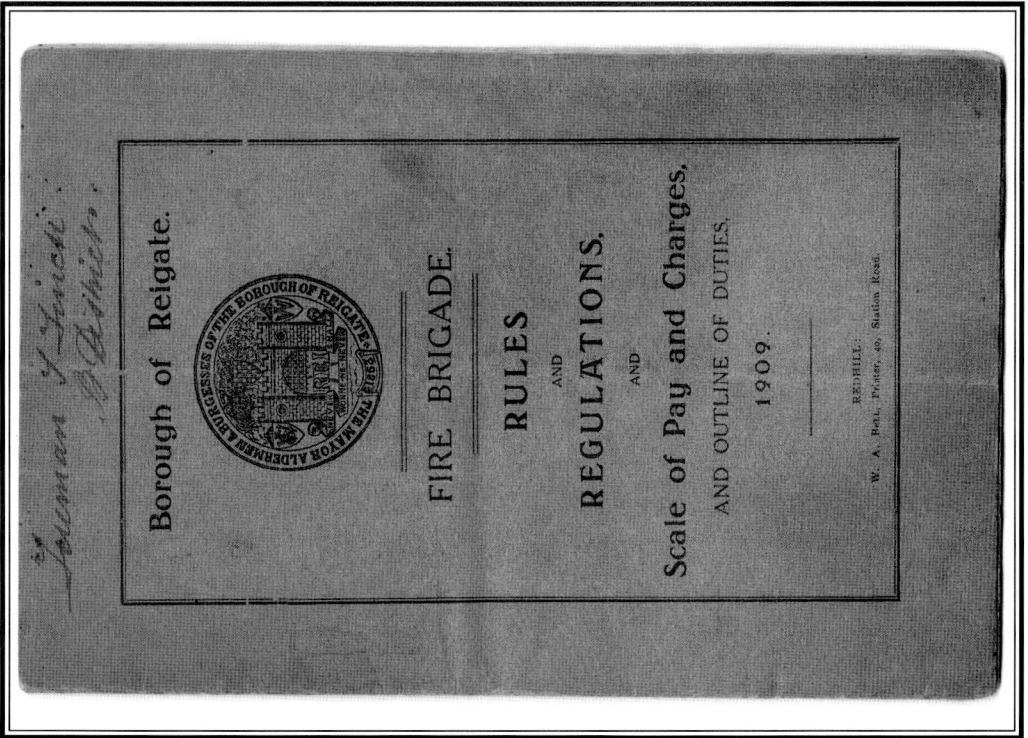

Rules and regulations of the Brigade 1909

Fire station open day 1908, with demonstration of live 'Carry Down' from station roof

Sear was appointed in his place at 25/- per week plus emoluments.

This was the closure of the episode of Reigate's first resident fireman but not the end of the story as far as Fireman Dean was concerned. Sutton Coldfield's Chief Officer had resigned in March, 1909, but had remained in charge for a further four years. Probably he was not a full-time officer, for on 17th February, 1913, the Sutton Coldfield authorities had decided to employ a full-time man who could drill the men and generally improve efficiency. They advertised and Fireman Dean became Chief Officer Dean on 14th July, 1913. His pay was thirty shillings per week (5/- more than at Reigate) plus a house, the latter presumably an improvement on the rooms over the Reigate HQ.

All that is known of his elevated Fire Brigade career is that during WW1 he made a request to his new authority for permission to employ any person at a fire caused by enemy action. The reply is unknown. By September, 1928, his wage had risen to £208 per year but he must have felt he was worth more because he asked for an increase. It looks like this was the first time he met failure in such a request, of which he had made a few over the years, because there is no record of a reply being given. He resigned his post in April, 1929, and the irony is that his successor was appointed at £256 per year, a clear one pound a week more than Chief Officer Dean had been receiving, although there may have been a different set of circumstances as regards the provision of accommodation

It would be interesting to know more about Fireman/Chief Officer Dean. In 1910 he had qualified for a bronze medal and one bar for fifteen years service, so must have joined the brigade around 1895, which means that by 1929 his service would have totalled around thirty-four years.

Title and Premises
The following is taken from the 1909 Borough of Reigate Rules and Regulations and Scale of Pay and Charges and Outline of Duties.

Title
The Brigade shall be appointed by the Corporation and shall be called "THE BOROUGH OF REIGATE FIRE BRIGADE."

Head Quarters
The Head Quarters of the Brigade shall be at the Fire Station in the Municipal Buildings, Reigate.

List of Fire Stations
A. District.

A. Head Quarters	Fire Station		Municipal Buildings.
C. Meadvale	"	"	Somerset Road.
D. South Park	"	"	Allingham Road.

B. District.

B. Redhill Fire Station, Police Station.	
E. Earlswood Fire Station, Common Road.	

1909-1913 - Resignations
Although this history stated previously that, all in all, there was no evidence to suggest that the

amalgamation of the two Brigades in 1909 was anything but amicable, it is not entirely certain that all was a bed of roses. In April 1913 it was revealed in Council that since Captain Rouse had taken over there had been eighteen resignations from the force, a rather unusually high number.

The matter came to full official and public recognition when the Watch Committee recommended that Foreman William Hockett and Foreman John Green, having reached the age limit, should be informed that the committee did not think it advisable that they should continue their service in the Fire Brigade. Foreman Hockett had 38 years service and Foreman Green 12 years. Both were aged 50.

The Council disagreed. Two councillors moved and seconded that the recommendation be referred back, and another Councillor, Mr Ince, asked if there was any more to the recommendation that just age. He said that the question of resignations from the Brigade was one which the public generally had been noticing with some alarm. He pointed out that there were a number of men now in the Brigade with little or no experience at all, whilst the experienced men had left or been driven out, he did not know which.

Another Councillor supported the amendment to refer the matter back but Alderman Gilbert brought up the matter of a report on the subject prepared by Captain Rouse on a previous occasion when this matter had been raised, which fully answered all the queries on the matter. Alderman Gilbert made it clear that he supported the Chief Officer, and although the content of the report was not aired at this meeting Council Alderman Barnes said that the Council should pause before it discussed men's characters, thereby quite possibly giving a clue to its references.

The fact that the recommendation for these men to retire was that of Captain Rouse and not just the Watch Committee was now clear. Alderman Malcolmson said that the Chief Officer was justified in his actions. He had been brought in to re-organise the Brigade and the Alderman was sure that most Councillors would agree he had succeeded beyond their expectations. He had put the Brigade in first class condition; he had drilled the men so that they competed successfully with other brigades, and on the whole the Reigate Brigade was second to none in a borough of their description. In doing so Captain Rouse had probably spent more money than the Council cared for, but if they were to have an efficient Brigade that could be relied upon, then they had to pay for it. He thought the Chief Officer should be absolved from any of the negative aspects in the suggestions made; he had shown great consideration in many cases, and no doubt it had been necessary for him to take action at times.

The Mayor then read out a rule that stated that firemen should retire at the age of fifty, but that the Chief Officer, Superintendent's and Foreman's cases should be considered by the Watch Committee. The vote was taken and it seems that the Council was not convinced of the case for retirement as the vote confirmed that the matter was to be referred back.

Now it must be remembered that whilst there were paid posts in the Brigade the majority of the force was voluntary. This point was raised in a letter to a local paper from a ratepayer who signed himself merely 'Inquirer'.

'Sir, I should like to emphasise the question raised in Council by Mr Ince: "Is there anything more than the question of age behind the request that these men be asked to resign?" It may be thought that as the Brigade is voluntary we ratepayers have not the same interest in it, but when we realise that had we not the free services of these men then we should need paid services, we begin to inquire as to why we see so many instances of resignations. Mr Malcolmson talks first of justification of the actions of the Chief Officer, then that he has spent more money than the Council cared for. What does this mean? When it comes to asking men with 38 and 12 years service to resign we are puzzled. Is it not logical that in training others to take their places we incur more expenditure? And is it not so that a Brigade which is fre-

quently parting with the experienced for the non-experienced cannot be as efficient as one that retains the experienced? The Mayor read a rule which referred to Firemen, not Foremen, and it must be construed that there is some other reason why the committee did not express their appreciation of services rendered by retaining these men.'

Some very strong and valid points, but not strong nor valid enough for the Watch Committee which, at the next Council meeting, re-affirmed its decision that the two Foremen should retire.

Mr Ince was still not satisfied. Why was it, he asked, if the question of age was the reason for retirement, that only a few days previously Captain Rouse was making enquiries about putting Foreman Green on the telephone. The matter of a 'round robin', signed by three Brigade members, complaining of lack of attention to drills, that had been presented to Captain Rouse, was also raised. It was acting upon this that Captain Rouse had asked that Foreman Green's service not be continued, but although there had been six ordinary drills and five extra ones, Foreman Green had attended them all.

Instead of a clear answer to these questions the Chief Officer's report was finally produced. It detailed that the 18 causes of resignation were: Death 1 - ill-health 3 - age 4 - inability to attend drills 3 - left the district 3 - discipline 3 - dismissed 1. Alderman Malcolmson, the previous supporter of the Chief Officer, said that he had no knowledge of the 'round robin', and if a voluntary Brigade were not allowed to choose their officers where did the democratic principle come in? Why all the dispute, insinuation and innuendo when there was simply nothing in it? The Brigade was in a better position than it had ever been and the Council ought to give the Chief Officer credit for the work he had done and the efficiency he had brought the Brigade to. The Watch Committee's report was finally adopted.

So what are we to make of this apparent small blip in the smooth running of the Fire Brigade? A few possible answers suggest themselves: -
The Chief Officer was moulding the Brigade into one he could more easily and fully control by getting rid of any experienced and confident individuals who saw that he was not as good as he was cracked up to be and who might oppose him or influence others to do so.
He was getting rid of dead wood as part of creating an efficient force.
He was being manipulated by others in the Brigade who wanted the two Foremen out for their own reasons.
The Brigade had indeed raised its standards, but mainly in the area of drill. In order to raise standards further and produce a team capable of consistently beating teams from other forces, thereby making not only the Brigade look good but enabling himself to take the credit and justify his appointment, he had to get rid of old, slow and unfit men, however experienced, and replace them with younger, fitter, stronger and faster men.
The process was one of natural progress in a Brigade where inefficient management had been replaced an by efficient and forward looking Chief Officer.
There was, as Alderman Malcolmson had said, nothing in it.
Some other reason.

This is simply a list of possible circumstances as this history should remain apart from coming to any conclusion for which there is insufficient evidence. This does not mean that there in no evidence at all, however, for in the course of research an ex-1930s fireman of no small experience was interviewed. On the subject of Captain Rouse - to reduce colourful and powerfully expressed language to its basic meaning - he described him as totally useless and as not having a clue as to what he was about. This one-off opinion, while demonstrating that the Chief Officer was not universally admired, is not sufficient to make too much more of the matter other than remembering two points:

1) That earlier in this century class difference was far more apparent and emphatic than it is today, and the middle class in Reigate might have been overwhelmingly well represented in the Watch Committee, the Council in General, and by some of the heads of the local services,

2) That many, if not all, firemen would have been drawn from the working classes. This would have included all up to and including the rank of Superintendent, and it should be remembered that the Chief Officer was a bridge between the Watch Committee and the Brigades.

Having dealt thus far with the matter it ought now to remain where it was left in 1913, for while speculation can be interesting, and while it would be very enlightening to be able to fully and accurately assess the popularity of Captain Rouse, history is not hindsight, nor is it infallible, and opinion can be coloured by so many things that it is best to stick with known facts.

1913 - Social Duties

The Chief Officer had social duties to perform in addition to his more practical activities. He presided at annual dinners of the Brigade, led his men at the Mayor's church parades, attended and spoke at inter-brigade functions, attended some civic functions, and represented the Brigade at various other gatherings.

Brigade members and their hosts pose for the camera in the French Town of "Clichy"

At one function that was far from local, he attended not alone but with a contingent of men. This was a visit to the French town of Clichy, the date being Whitsun, 1913, the occasion the International Meeting of Fire Brigades. The Reigate Borough men gave a display of life saving from a drill tower and an exhibition of hose drill and ambulance work. They stayed at the local hotel and the following day were taken around the sights of Paris. They returned by the night boat, all expenses having been paid by the French town council.

The trip was not such a rare occurrence, Chief Officer Rouse, often accompanied by other fire chiefs, made several visits to the continent. Today there are still strong continental connections and firemen from Surrey regularly visit Belgium in a semi-official capacity and take part in the November 11th Menin Gate ceremony.

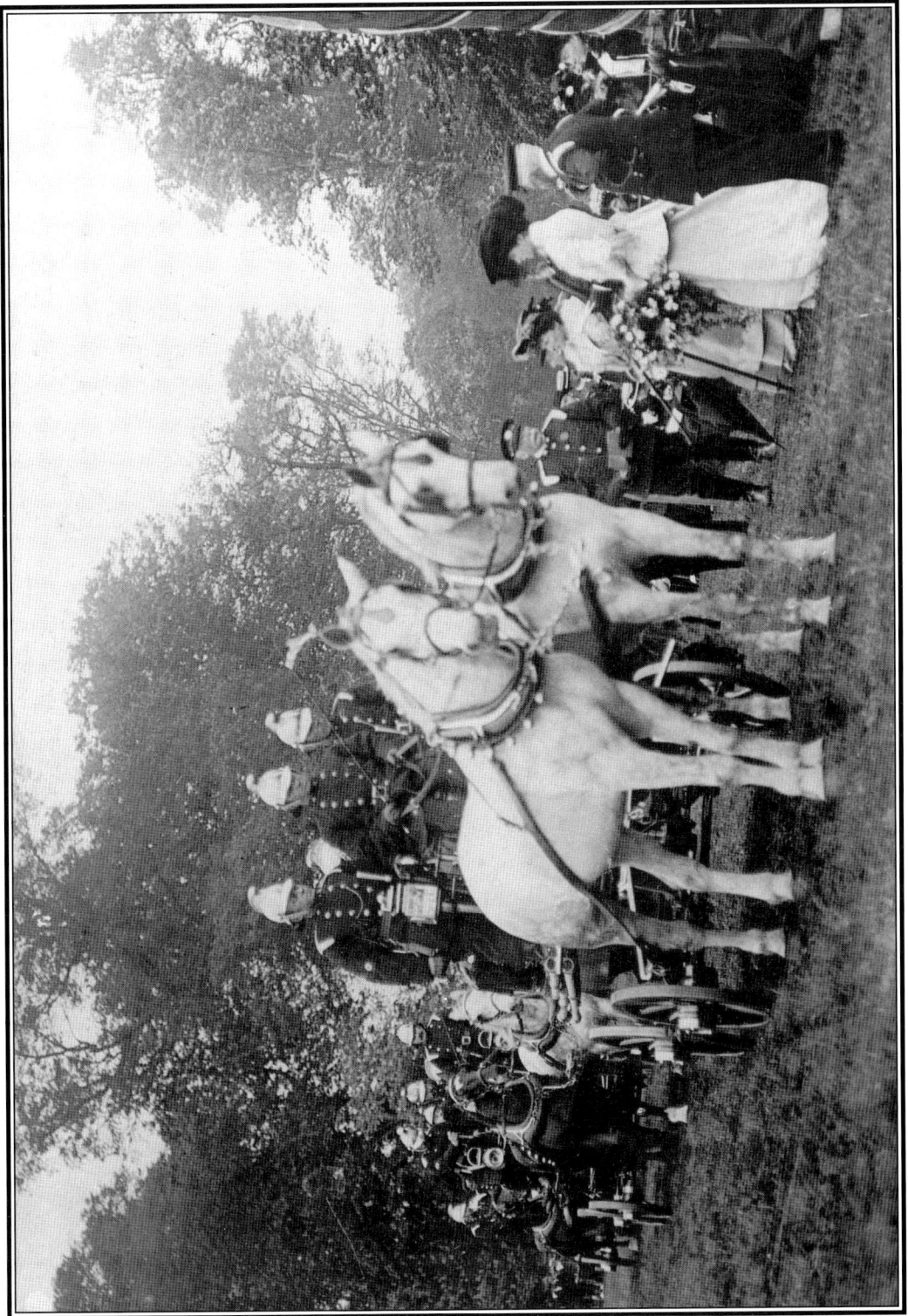

Taggs Island summer fete 1913

Another 1913 event was that of a Grand Fete held at Tagg's Island, the property of Mr Fred Karno. This involved the gathering of 150 men from 39 brigades of Surrey and Middlesex and their inspection by the Earl of Londesborough. The Earl was accompanied by his wife, the Countess, and they were conducted along the ranks by Captain Rouse. The Countess wore a dress of cream chignon and a large white hat with pink flowers, she must have made quite a contrast with the paraded men in their dark uniforms and shining helmets. After the inspection the firemen lined up at the landing stage where a 'pageant' of people impersonating Queen Elizabeth and other English aristocracy, 'sailed' up in a mock-up of a state barge. They disembarked for speeches and a display by Hampton firemen of the advantage of the modern machine (described as a 'weird contrivance with an upright boiler') over the bucket and hand squirt.

The event sounds like a non-starter today but attracted large crowds. It was staged as a fund raising event for the National Fire Brigades Union Widows and Orphans Fund and £130 was raised.

1911 - The Case of Henry Laker

In 1911 there was an episode concerning an insurance agent for the Prudential who was also a fireman. James Henry Laker, a married man living at Allingham Road, South Park, Reigate, and a member of the Reigate Brigade, was found dead on the railway line close to the Croydon Road Bridge. At the subsequent coroner's enquiry it came to light that although he had appeared cheerful on the morning of the day of his death he had money worries.

Funeral of J. H. Laker

In a letter written shortly before his death Mr Laker referred to his Fire Assurance Superintendent and Assistant Superintendent as being bloodsuckers, and there was another reference to eighteen months arrears. Evidence at the enquiry showed that he was fully paid up to that January, however, and also that he had also been worried by a feeling that he was going mad and would have to go into an asylum.

The full truth of the matter was not something the enquiry had to deal with as it was concerned simply with ascertaining the cause of death, which it did by returning a verdict of 'Suicide during temporary insanity'. A newspaper article later took up the story, expressing concerns about the fact that there was possibly a situation existing whereby the agent was expected to make up out of his own pocket any contributions uncollected, and that if a policy was to lapse because of this then it was a very serious matter for Mr Laker.

James Laker was buried with full Brigade honours, his coffin being carried on a fire engine covered with a Union Jack. On it were placed the deceased's medals, helmet and axe. A large crowd lined the route from the Municipal Buildings to the Reigate Parish Church. The procession was headed by a small detachment of the Reigate Borough Police followed by the Reigate Priory Band. After these came the main body of mourners and behind them the Reigate Borough Brigade in full uniform under the command of Chief Officer Rouse accompanied by Supt. Allison of the London Salvage Corps, Superintendents Mason and Legg from Redhill and Reigate respectively, Chief Officers Lockhart from Merstham, Gibson from Charlwood and Stovell from Betchworth. The presence of Supterintendent Allison of the London Salvage Corps might have been because the LSC was run by the insurance companies.

1911 - Chimney Fires
Having a fire is one thing but having a fire for which he property owner is seen to be responsible for, and in breach of the law, is another. Such was the case for chimney fires, it being judged that if the chimney was on fire then the cause was sooting up, a situation preventable by regular sweeping.

Reports in the press of people being taken to court and fined for allowing their chimney to catch alight were fairly commonplace. The bare facts of some of the cases were reported in the local press; some of those from 1911 are reproduced here:

Alexander Ball, London road, Redhill, summoned for allowing a chimney to be on fire, was mulcted (fined) *in the sum of 2s 6d. - Samuel Landan, 66, High Street, Redhill, summoned for a like offence, was fined 5s. including costs. George King, Nutley Lane, Reigate, was similarly summoned. Fireman Jeal, who gave evidence, said the fire caused the chimney of the adjoining house to be set on fire. Defendant said he had the chimneys at his house swept four times to the once of those of his neighbour on either side. Asked the cause of the fire he said he put it down to bad sweeping. A fine of 5s. including costs was imposed.*

William Wenman of Clarendon Road, Redhill, was summoned for allowing the chimney at his house to be on fire. PC Green deposed as to the facts of the case and a penalty of 2s 6d. was imposed.

A chimney fire could happen to anyone at almost any time unless the chimney was absolutely clean and sweeps must have found a good friend in this law. Reports of the court appearances and the results were not very imposing journalism perhaps, but served to warn others of the financial penalties involved, and possibly got them running round to their local soot shifter.

Such were the difficulties of a bygone age.

Notes for Chapter Four
[1] *Source: Fred Legg's Reports and Applications book of 1903*

[2] *Source - Newspaper article in Fred Legg's report book*

[3] *At this time, however, due to the fact that Redhill did not then exist, the provision of the two engines by their lordships, and the formation of crews to 'practice' them, was also at a time when there was only one Fire Brigade.*

[4] *Could this have been the one that Reigate never sold?*

[5] *Pompier ladders were ladders using a toothed hook at the top end to smash through window glass and to anchor on a sill, enabling a fireman to climb up to the next floor. They were the Continental version of the British hook ladder and it may be that Reigate favoured them because Chief Officer Rouse had frequent connections with, and made frequent visits to, the French and Belgian Brigades. Such ladders are no longer in use in this country.*

Chapter Five

Towards the Modern Era

Motorisation

During the formative years of the 20th century there were the beginnings of a radical movement away from the use of horses as prime movers of all kinds of vehicles, including fire engines. At the time it was possibly seen by some of those who had been used to horsepower in its literal form for the whole of their lives as no more than an interesting and rather special addition to the appliances under their control. They may have seen the noise and fumes produced as serious disadvantages, and possibly reacted, as many do, with an apparently natural pessimism about 'new fangled' machinery that is always connected with change and often connected with fewer jobs.

There were many others, not least the manufacturers, who saw these new machines as not just a passing fad but as the way forward, with advantages that would prove themselves in the fullness of time.

Around the turn of the century the self-propelled steamer had been a fairly new addition to the family of fire fighting machinery but the motorised engine was on its way. The first self-propelled motor fire engine had been purchased in 1901 by Eccles Borough Council. It had no pump or escape but was a tender with the capacity to carry men and equipment. In trials it achieved fourteen mph fully loaded, its main difficulties being hold-ups due to sheep and cattle on the roads. It went into use but proved, at seven horsepower, to be under powered.

Liverpool Fire Service also bought a motor tender in the same year; it was a larger and more substantial version which could carry a fair sized crew. Liverpool took delivery of a Daimler motor the following year upon which was fitted a sixty-gallon chemical engine before the vehicle was subjected to extensive trials. Fitted with an open flame ignition system that caused misfiring it was christened 'Farting Annie' by the Brigade. It was considered unsuitable for a first turnout appliance and was relegated to use as a stores tender.

These less than wholly successful early machines were succeeded by a twenty horsepower engine at Tottenham in 1904 and a thirty horsepower pump at Finchley in 1905. Both proved adequate for the tasks they were designed to perform and were sensations at the time. Reliability was something that only time would confirm and conservative brigades continued to order the new self-propelled steamer and the much older, horse-drawn manuals.

Reliability was not one hundred per cent for any machine and a feature of the promotion of motorised equipment was comparison of speed and efficiency with older designs of equipment. The result was said to have been the demise of the self-propelled steamer within five years of its inception, and the eventual disuse of the horsed steamers and manual engines, but some were still in use on private estates at the beginning of the second World War. The firm of Merryweather actually produced some steamers for the military between 1939 and 45. These were of 1890 design but could be operated on any kind of fuel available.

There was a trial of a motorised fire escape tender at Reigate on a Saturday morning in 1912. The machine was a 35hp four cylinder, vertical engined machine built by J and E Hall Ltd of Dartford. It had a 3-speed gearbox, weighed 2 tons 14 cwt, and besides a 40 ft escape ladder could carry 2,500 feet of hose. On hand to see a demonstration around Reigate was the Mayor, Mr. F.E.Lemon, the Town Clerk, Mr Alfred Smith, Chief Officer Captain Rouse and Mr E.S.Gedge.

There were a number of occasions when calls for motorisation had been made. Very close to the time of this demonstration there was a very bad fire at Foster's Temperance Hotel at the top of the Brighton Road, near to the Cutting. There had been a delay while the horsed escape and water tower was sent for and subsequently brought from Reigate fire station and run up to the front of the building and, with other hoses, had attacked the fire. The fire was overcome but not before the top half of the building was almost a complete loss. Newspaper reports noted that had there been an escape and water tower at Redhill the fire would have been contained more quickly and less damage done. It was further suggested that a motor turbine escape would have been even better, being able to reach any part of the Borough much more speedily.

No immediate purchase resulted, however, and an early 1913 newspaper article on the subject argued for motorisation as follows: -

MOTOR FIRE ENGINES

Wimbledon is the latest district to supply itself with motor fire engines; and it will probably not be many years before the horsed fire engine almost everywhere will be relegated to the museum along with the last of the hansom cabs. The advantages of the motor-propelled vehicle for fire-service are very great. The rapidity with which they can be turned out and cover the distance to the seat of a fire alone establishes them in the favour of practical men, and must continue to do so. As fire fighting machines also they are very powerful; they excel again in this respect. There is the single question of their reliability which is apt to give pause, and that does not disturb owners of the best type of machine. In towns like Kingston and Wimbledon - in both of which, by the way, the Dennis engine built at Guildford, has been adopted - rich enough to duplicate their fire-engines, the chance of accidental stoppage or delay from causes which occasionally affect even the best regulated motor-vehicles has been reduced to a minimum, the doubling of the plant protecting them against that risk, whatever it be; and it does also bring nearer the day when the smaller districts, whose requirements are met by a single fire-engine, can look forward to exchanging the horse-drawn for the motor-propelled vehicle. With Kingston and Wimbledon already supplied with two power-driven motor-engines apiece, and Surbiton likely soon to follow suit, the risk to be run by any of the intervening or outlying districts which may contemplate the installation of a single motor-engine is infinitesimal. Indeed, were the whole area one for fire-fighting purposes it is possible to conceive the strategic placing of fire-engine machines so as to render considerable economies possible. But that is only by the way. The point is that with the larger towns so powerfully equipped, the smaller ones knowing, as they have always known, that in the hour of emergency they can ever rely upon the assistance of their neighbours, may see their way to adopt the motor-driven machine earlier than at present appears possible or prudent to some of them.

Later in the year there was a tiny piece at the bottom of a report on Council proceedings which read simply:

Fred Legg and crew pose for the camera with their new 1914 Dennis

PROPOSED MOTOR FIRE TENDER

*The Watch Committee recommended that the Chief Officer of the Fire
Brigade should fully report as to the advisability of obtaining a motor
tender for the use of the Borough. The report was adopted.*

At the dinner following the annual competition later in 1913 quite a bit was said on the subject in the speeches. Guest Captain Dane, Chief Officer of the Croydon Fire Brigade, commented that Reigate had a very nice fire station but it would look a lot better if it housed motor appliances. It was hard on horses to cover the whole of the 6,000 acres of the Borough. The fire protection of the town would be substantially increased by the provision of a machine.

After further speeches and toasts Captain Rouse got his chance to add to the debate on the matter of motorisation. He said that the Reigate Fire Brigade had its duty to carry out, but so did the Town Council, and maintaining the efficiency of the Brigade formed an important part of this duty. He added that this was jubilee year (the Borough, formed in 1863, was 50 years old) but the jubilee of the old manual engines had been reached long since.

This statement was not entirely accurate, as Captain Rouse well knew, for only the previous year, in his 1912 report to the Watch Committee (already reported in this history but worth repeating) he had noted that: *'Both manuals have had to be repaired on several occasions. The manual in 'A' district was built in 1857 and the manual in 'B' in 1865 and both are showing the effects of age and hard work.* So one had been 50 years old in 1907 but in 1913 the other still had two years to go until its jubilee.

The Captain continued, saying that at the present time there were towns of a quarter Reigate's size (28,502 in 1911 census) possessing up-to-date equipment. No town, he added, had more loyal servants that the members of the Borough Brigade - plenty of 'hear, hears' (terms of agreement never missed in newspaper reports of the day) at this sentiment.

The Town Council's mind on the matter was finally made up in December of 1913 when the Watch Committee passed a resolution that the time had come when a first-aid motor tender should be provided for the Borough. (The term 'first-aid' referred to a vehicle carrying a hose reel) It recommended that the Chief Officer's specification for such a vehicle, as already presented, be approved, and that tenders for its provision be invited.

Curiously, part of the specification was that the vehicle was to carry 100 gallons of chemicals, rather than water, the reason put forward being that the latter caused considerable damage at fires whereas the chemicals did as good a job with less damage. This reveals ignorance on someone's part as the so-called 'chemicals' were 95% water anyway, so were no better as far as damage caused was concerned.

The cost was to be borne by a loan, payments to be spread over five years and a group of four men, comprising the Mayor, the Chief Officer, Alderman Apted and Alderman Gilbert, were deputed to visit other fire stations recently in possession of a motorised fire appliance, and to report their findings back to the committee at a later date.

In 1914 the Borough's first motor engine, a Dennis escape tender, was acquired. Previously a Bailey horsed escape had been in use. Dennis had been selling their motor appliances for some years, in the south of England to Kingston in 1910, Wimbledon in 1912 and Guildford and Egham in 1913.

The first serious use of the new Reigate appliance was the following year, 1915, at a fire at the Athenaeum printing works in Brighton Road, Redhill. A local resident, Mrs Martin, interviewed in

1992, recalled the glass of the windows of the nearby cottage in which she lived as a girl, melting from the heat generated at this winter blaze. This 1914 Dennis was still giving good service in the 1930s, when it had its solid tyres replaced by pneumatics.

Advertisement for Reigate's new Dennis Light 6 prior to outbreak of the Second Would War

Roll of Honour

of the Members of the Borough of Reigate Fire Brigade who served in the Great War, 1914-1918.

Rank.	Name.	Rank.	Unit or Ship.	Casualties.
Chief Officer	... G, C. M. Rouse	Major	... Royal Munster Fusiliers...	... Mentioned in Despatches.
District Officer	... M. Whitmore	Corporal	... Royal Defence Corps ...	... —
,, ,,	... A. Whitmore	Staff-Sergt....	Royal Army Service Corps	... —
Sub-Officer	... W. H. Jeal ...	Lc/Cpl.	... Royal Garrison Artillery	... —
,,	... C. Winchester	Gunner	... Royal Garrison Artillery	... —
,, ...	... C. Piggott ...	1st Class P.O.	*H.M.S. Editor*, Mine Sweeper	... —
★Ambulance Instr....	W. Smith ...	King's Cpl.	2nd Life Guards (Inf.) ...	... Killed
Fireman ...	... C. Baker ...	Private	... Royal Army Medical Corps	... Torpedoed.
,, ...	... W. Charman...	Lc/Cpl.	... 24th County of London	... Gassed.
,, ...	... C. Chapman	Driver	... Royal Field Artillery ...	... —
Coachman	... J. Coomes ...	Driver	... Royal Army Service Corps	... —
Fireman ...	... B. Burbridge	Driver	... Royal Army Service Corps	... —
,,	... E. Easton ...	A.B. Seaman	*H.M.S. Dunscombe* ...	Torpedoed (2)
,,	... J. Greenough	Sergeant	... 5th Bn. The Queen's Regt.	... —
,,	... G. Hockett ...	Driver	... R.A.S.C. Motor Transport	... —
,,	... A. Humphery	Gunner	... Royal Garrison Artillery	... —
,,	... F. Legg, Junr.	2/Lt. Pilot	... 4th Queens, attchd. R.A.F.	... Wounded.
,,	... G. Legg ...	Private	... Kings Royal Rifle Corps	... —
,,	... F. Mackrell ...	Sapper	... Royal Engineers	... Wounded & Prisoner of War.
,, ...	... P. Poat ...	Driver	... Royal Engineers	... Wounded.
Coachman	... H. Porter ...	Driver	... Royal Army Service Corps	... —
Fireman ...	... C. Smith ...	Driver	... R.A.S.C. Motor Transport	... Wounded.
,,	... H. Topliss ...	Corporal	... R.A.S.C., Canteen Section	... —
,,	... C. Willett ...	Lc/Cpl.	... Royal Army Medical Corps	... Gassed.
,,	... F. Winchester	Private	... 5th Bn. The Queens Regt.	... —
,,	... E. Winchester	Driver	... R.A.S.C. Motor Transport	... —
,,	... A. Winchester	Private	... Tank Corps	... Injured.
★ ,, ...	... S. Woodhouse	Sapper	... Royal Engineers	... Killed.
,,	... G. Wickens ...	Private	... Grenadier Guards ...	... —
,,	... F. Walker ...	Mechanic	...·Royal Air Force ...	... —
,,	... A. Ware ...	Corporal	... Machine Gun Corps ...	...Wounded (2)
,,	... C. Whitmore	Private	... 5th Bn. The Queen's Regt.	... —
,,	... H. Young ...	Sergeant	... 5th Bn. The Queen's Regt.	... —
,·	... G. Young ...	Sergeant	... 5th Bn. The Queen's Regt.	... —

*Roll of Honour 1914-18 First World War. *(See page 139 and 140)*

1914-1918 - The Great War

August 4th 1914 saw the beginning of the First World War. Captain Rouse was a reserve officer and so was called up for active service. Superintendent F.Legg replaced him as acting Chief Officer. In all, thirty-five members of the local Brigade were to end up in His Majesty's Service.

During the war, in 1917, a munitions train was found to be alight at Redhill station. The subsequent successful operation to contain and extinguish the fire resulted in F.Legg winning the OBE, a medal that for many years was proudly owned by his son, Sherry Legg, who said that if anyone addressed his father verbally or in writing, including his OBE suffix, he would always state in no uncertain terms that the medal, although awarded to him, was won by the whole of his fire team on duty at the fire that day.

Captain Rouse had been gazetted a Captain in the Royal Munster Fusiliers shortly after the outbreak of war and had been appointed a Staff Captain at on GHQ staff in Ireland. In addition he had been appointed Inspector of Fire Services to the Irish Command. He was mentioned in despatches in 1916 and 1919 and was promoted to Major in 1923 on retirement, when he resumed his duties as Chief Officer of the Reigate Borough Fire Brigade. As a result of war experience a siren was placed on the Reigate tower. Its sound was heard over a long distance and it called in men who might be absent from their homes when they were needed.

Reigate Borough Brigade's first motorised engines

1923 - The End of the Manuals

In 1923 a 250-gallon motor pump was purchased. It was fitted with a 'Talmene' turbine pump and signalled the end for the old manual engines, which ceased use in 1924, thereby ending an era which had lasted an amazing one hundred and fifteen years. One wonders how many horses had been used to pull these four engines throughout this period. Many horses had been lost in the war, of course, and with the rise of motorised vehicles their use was in decline anyway. In fact their falling numbers had meant that horses had been proving difficult to obtain for Fire Brigade use, so the transfer to motor power was inevitable. With these new vehicles the delay of horsing the old engines became a thing of the past, and with their superior speed it meant that their attendance time was so good that the sub-stations were able to be done away with.

Not all manual engines were consigned to the scrap heap, however. In some rural parts of the country some of them were dusted off as late as the Second World War and pressed into service to fight air-raid fires.

Fred Legg and crew aboard their new Dennis fire pump c1924

1932 - A New Station for Redhill

The siting of separate fire stations in each of the two towns of Reigate and Redhill was a policy that never wavered until the setting up of a single (more or less central) station at St Davids, Reigate, in the 1950s. The notion of a centralised police station, on the other hand, was one which was considered from the very earliest days of the Borough force, and half an acre of land was purchased from Mr Alfred James Waterlow in October, 1864, for the very purpose. The proposal to do so was carried by the casting vote of the Mayor, and perhaps the fairly equal division of opinion on the matter was the reason why nothing was done. The land lay unoccupied until 1870 when Mr Waterlow agreed to take back the land, the plan having finally foundered in favour of a police station in each town.

If this six-year story of the 'centralised' police station of the nineteenth century could be considered to be drawn out, then the story of the 'new' fire station at Redhill is quite a saga by comparison. It began only one year later than the police station non-event, in 1865, when Redhill's Fire Brigade was first formed. There had to be a permanent home for the new town's fire engine, and in a motion proposed by Councillor Young at a Council meeting of 9th September of that year, it was proposed

Redhill's new fire station 1932

'that the Watch Committee be empowered to carry into effect their recommendation as to a watch house and lock-up cells at Warwick Town to include a shed for the fire engines and water carts at a cost not to exceed £400'.

As already stated, one of the first tasks the new Council had set itself was to form its own police force and although this had been done, probably because of the uncertainty about where to locate it, a proper police station in the town had not yet been built. The watch house and cells rectified this situation and the opportunity was being taken to house the fire engine at the same time. The contract was awarded to one Thomas Penfold for the erection of the said watch house and cells and presumably included a fire shed. The work finished in May, 1865.

There was a snag. Access to the new engine shed was too narrow and alternative site had to be found. Why this had not been foreseen is unclear but the chosen alternative location was Mr Topliss's coach house in West Street (later renamed Cromwell Road) Redhill.

How long the engine was housed there is unknown but the cost to the Borough Council was £12 per annum, payable half yearly, a considerable sum in those days, and equal to the annual wages of the salaried members of the Fire Brigade of that time. Its next move was to Chalmers and Wood's High Street showrooms, or attached accommodation. The date of the move is unknown but the engine was still housed there when William Hockett joined the force in 1875. [1] In 1884 the Corporation received a notice from Chalmers and Wood to quit the fire engine room in the High Street. It was put in the hands of the Mayor, Mr Field, to find a new location, but the problem was temporarily resolved by Chalmers and Wood granting a six-month extension to their quit notice.

Clearly it was necessary to station the engine in or close to the centre of the town. The largest undeveloped area at the time was the south-east quadrant where the Market Field was. This had been bought from the railway company years before and was the property of the Market Hall

Company. That body was approached in March of 1885 to see what its terms would be for a suitable piece of ground. In August of 1886 the Town Clerk was being instructed to apply to the Market Hall Company for the very same reason, so either nothing had been done in the meantime of negotiations were very slow. In that October the Surveyor's plans for a building to be erected on such a site were forwarded to the Market Hall Co. The Council expressed its willingness to either lease or buy the land.

In January of 1887 a letter was received by the Corporation from a Mr Grimes offering land for a new engine shed. There was a Mr Grimes who had a furniture store on the west side of the High Street between Chapel and Lower Bridge Roads in the 1880s [2] and this offer was possibly from the same man. This came to nothing, however, as another option had emerged. The Council already owned land alongside the Market Hall where as previously related, years before they had erected a police station and an inaccessible engine shed. It now appeared that if they could negotiate a right of way over adjacent land they could build a new engine room there. The adjacent land, owned by Mr Hunt, stretched from the eastern side of the Market Hall, probably with the exception of the Corporation land, all the way to Ladbroke Road, and success in the matter solved the access problem, although the way was still fairly narrow.

Tenders for the erection of a fire engine house were received from nine contractors. Prices ranged from a high of £161 to the lowest of £105. This latter considerably undercut the others and it was resolved to accept it subject to a schedule of prices passing scrutiny. As it turned out this tender was abandoned and the tender of a Mr W.H.Cook accepted at the next price of £124.

By June, 1887, fittings were being procured for the new engine house. These included 25 feet of shelves, nails and pegs for the south side, a piece of india rubber pipe to attach to the tap for washing the engine, a 3ft by 7ft table, two benches and two chairs plus a cupboard with a lock. Functionality, not luxury, was the order of the day. In addition, tenders were sought for wrought iron gates to guard the entrance to the site. Redhill firm Lanaway and Son's bid of £7-10 was successful. The new building was insured for £100, the fire engine for £250, and the hoses and other appliances for a further £100.

The question arises, where was the engine kept between quitting Chalmers in 1884/5 and occupying the new premises. The answer is given in a 1913 Surrey Mirror article on William Hockett's retirement, which states that it was kept in the Market Field until the new premises were ready.

All would now seem to be fine - but not so. The ground on which the new station had been built also contained the police station (what had happened to the original engine shed built with it in 1866 is not known) and accommodation there had become inadequate by 1893. In that December a five-man sub-committee of the Watch Committee was set up to *investigate and report on the best means of providing a remedy for the insufficient accommodation at Redhill Police Station.* The sub-committee was comprised of Mayor Budgen, Alderman Markham and Councillors Brooks, Ongley and Farringdon, and the following February they recommended that: *accommodation be made in the Market Hall for the Head Constable and that a station be provided for the Redhill fire engine and appliances.*

This does not make full sense in the context of what had gone before. Why should a new station be provided when just that had been done in 1887? The answer is probably that this second fire engine house was almost as unsatisfactory as the first (1866) one, in which case someone had to be responsible for incompetence or gross misdirection of Council funds, or both, if not worse. In the event the full Council did not approve the recommendation.

In March the Watch Committee resolved: *that the surveyor prepare a specification and estimate for the consideration of this committee for constructing four new cells at Redhill Police Station and converting the present residence into police offices.* Once again the Committee's resolve was not matched by that of the full Council, which asked that the Committee be requested: *'to consider and report upon the possibility of pulling down the present structure and erecting on the site police offices, offices for Weights and Measures, police cells and residence for the Head Constable.'* No mention this time of the Fire Station, which is more in line with the site really being unsuitable for that purpose.

Whatever was in the resultant report it is certain that nothing came from it.

The situation was overtaken by other events, when in May 1898 there was recorded in the Watch Committee minutes the following: *'Resolved that this committee recommend the council to meet the requirements of the Home Office by building a fire station, police station and residence for the Head Constable upon land to be acquired of Lady Somerset.'*.

This resolution was to result in magnificent new Reigate premises for the Corporation, the police and the fire brigade. This eased the situation at Redhill because the Head Constable would move to Reigate and vacate space which could be used to ease cramped conditions at Redhill. The Reigate facilities were commenced around 1900 and the Reigate firemen moved in to their new station on March 22nd 1902. Moving costs were £1.6.0 for the men's time, 5/- for horse, van and driver, and 7s.6d for horses for the engine.

This left room for Redhill to get back on the agenda. In May 1902, nine years after the original proposal for a sub-committee, it was resolved that: *'Councillors Condle, Brackley and Markham be a sub-committee to find a suitable site for the fire station at Redhill'* - same sub-committee but different members, and no mention this time of the police station. In light of this resolution it is clear that whilst everything had been achieved at Reigate, nothing had been achieved at Redhill.

And nothing was achieved by this new sub-committee either because in March of the following year, 1903, a further resolution stated that: *'a sub-committee of the Mayor, Alderman Viall and Councillors Reader and Saunders be appointed to find a new site for the fire and police station at Redhill.'*

In February, 1904, there was a letter to the Watch Committee from the Redhill Captain, John Mason, about the poor condition of Redhill fire station but no repairs were put in hand. Instead, in May 1905, there was another resolution: *'To recommend the Council pull down the present fire and police stations at Redhill and to erect new buildings on the site.'* Here, after a period of twelve years, was a repeat of the Council's own recommendation of 1893 to the Watch Committee, rebounding like an echo that had been lost for a rather long time.

Whether new buildings were provided is unknown. If they were they could not have proved much better than the old and it is probable that the old buildings remained just as they were. In 1908 the Town Clerk was instructed to communicate with the agents of Lord Monson to see if a site could be obtained for the Redhill fire and police station. This was the start of negotiations with Mssrs Mole, Rosling and Vernon in which both sides jockeyed for position. The Monson estate lands were usually sold on 99-year term leases, in fact almost the whole of Redhill was Monson land under leasehold. Most of these leases were 50 years old and the land in question was already leased and reversion monies would have to be paid as a consequence. Compounding the situation was the fact that much of the land was leased, split up and sub-leased to others. But, unlike in 1886, the Council now wanted to own the land outright and would have no other agreement than the land be freehold. A piece of land in London Road was identified that had a frontage of 75 feet and a depth of 200 feet.

Then, in October, 1908, there came an alternative suggestion. This was from the Market Hall Company and entailed a swap of the existing site for land on the Market Field with a cash adjustment of £200 - more echoes of twenty-odd years before. This was accepted only to be was rescinded the following March by the full Council, which instructed the Watch Committee that no bartering of land be entertained, only sterling values to be considered. That was the end of that, and in

May, 1909, came the end, it seemed, of the original negotiations, when it was resolved *'that the proposal to purchase land in London Road cannot be entertained'*.

So, in 1910, the familiar sub-committee was appointed once more *'for finding a suitable site for a new police and fire station'*. Its members were to be no more successful than their predecessors, and in 1911 there was a letter from Superintendent Mason (no longer a Captain following the appointment of Major Rouse as Chief Officer) again complaining about the state of the Redhill fire station. Also there were problems with surface water in front of the station and drainage work had to be put in hand.

A letter from Peat and Holdsworth, who were probably solicitors acting for the Monson estate, to this 1911 sub-committee about land came to nothing, as did a letter from L.Rees of Station Road to a subsequent 1912 sub-committee. Then, in June, 1912, there was another letter from Mole, Rosling and Vernon about the original London Road land, but it was still leasehold and their offer was rejected. Clearly this was a last attempt to sell the land under the familiar and usual leasehold arrangements - testing the Council's 1909 resolve and finding it firm - and the leasehold clause was dropped. A 1912 newspaper article reported on the subject as follows:

> *'The Watch Committee, reporting as to the negotiations for a site for a Police and Fire Station in the London Road, Redhill, recommended that the Corporation agree that the price to be paid Lord Monson for the land as freehold should not exceed £750.*
>
> *The Town Clerk read a letter from Mr C.Mole, stating that Lord Monson agreed to the suggestion which had been made, with certain stipulations. The sub committee of the Watch committee, inter alia, recommended that there should be a condition that the council should build within six feet of the southern boundary. Alderman Barnes said that the difficulty of finding a site had been enormous. The recommendations of the committee and sub-committee were accepted.'*

By November members of the Watch Committee were viewing the site and making further stipulations. These were that the council were to have unfettered rights to build within six feet of the boundary and that there were to be no covenants or stipulations to prevent them building the structure for the purposes they had in mind, to wit the police and fire station. It looked as though things were really moving. In December they were asking for purchase of additional land *'northwards to the stream'*, [3] extending the frontage to 97 feet.

In January, 1913, terms set out by Lord Monson's agents were approved subject to two points:
   a) *That the condition that no building be erected within 20 feet of the southern boundary be applicable only for a depth of 75-80 feet from the London Road.*
   b) *That the condition about the building line being altered so that the Corporation should not be compelled to set back the building beyond the frontage of the two adjoining houses on the south side of the site.*

This must have been agreed for by February there was a draft agreement drawn up and by May it was resolved that the agreement be approved and sealed. This was followed later in the year by another newspaper article reporting a recommendation of a loan for £1,100 for the Redhill fire and police station, £650 of the money for the police station and the remainder of £450 for the fire station. It was a recommendation that was adopted and procedures put in hand to borrow the money.

A Local Government Inquiry Board was set up in January 1914 to look into the application of the Reigate Corporation to borrow this sum. At this enquiry the Town Clerk stated that the period of the loan would be thirty years. The police station dated from 1866 and although the fire station was of much later date it was no more than two sheds, the front just sufficient to house the engine, the rear measuring 8' by 7', hardly sufficient for other appliances. The problem was exacerbated by the narrowness of the access. The council had had to make grooves for the wheels of the engine to run along and the walls had needed to be cut away to allow room for the wheelhubs to pass through. When the engine was out it then had to be turned around before it could be horsed, adding to the delay. He added that if the buildings could be pulled down and rebuilt there was still insufficient room, which was a pity because the land belonged to the council freehold.

Chief Officer Rouse [4] was less polite about the fire station, saying that it was not a fire station at all but two tumble-down sheds. Several others spoke in favour of the proposal, agreeing to a man that the new site was a very good one. No one seems to have spoken against and the inquiry closed.

The overall plan must have been further approved because contracts were finally exchanged in June, twenty and a half years after the first sub-committee had been formed to improve the situation at Redhill, twenty-seven years after the 'new' station had been built, and forty-eight years after the first, inaccessible, engine shed had been erected.

A competition was launched for a suitable design for the new police and fire station. This was won in 1914 by architect Mr Sunlight. The scheme was abandoned during the war but afterwards the plans were redesigned to include baths, and the fire and police stations were made smaller as a result. Even so, serious work on the project did not begin until 1928, the Mayor saying that the Council was anxious to get the project completed as soon as possible. Unfortunately the architect, who was still the original Mr Sunlight, now told the Council of the possibility of running sand beneath the peat bog on the site, raising the spectre of £600-700 extra expenditure on the foundations. Mr Worley of the Council seemed not to be surprised, saying that shifting sand was found when the South Eastern Hotel had been built. Also, when the excavation for the electricity transformer was made in the Market Place they had all the experts in the country there to advise how to put the first lot of concrete in because of the conditions.

The saga was due to continue for a little while longer as during construction water, especially after heavy rain, forced its way into the basement between the edge of the floor and the walls, necessitating the provision of a concrete raft over the basement floor at extra cost. At the opening ceremony Alderman Crosfield joked that other than the ratepayers everyone would be pleased with what they found in the building. He said they had an overflow at Reigate baths (a reference to excessive public demand to use its facilities and not seemingly an intended pun) that would be eased now Redhill baths were operative.

Much more could be said about the building of the baths because it was this part of the project that attracted most attention, almost as if the police and fire stations were an afterthought, when in fact it was the other way around. The whole of the engineering work regarding the filtration and hot water and steam plant, plus the heating of the building, as well as the supply of hot water and heating to the police and fire stations and all electrical work and installation, was carried out by Tamplin and Makovski. A siren was provided for the police and fire station (presumably to call out retained firemen) and the long delayed opening took place on Saturday 21st May 1932. The fire station was taken into commission on 11th July, 1933, bringing that town well and truly into the 20th century, and updating it in line with the similar provision, 30 years before, at Reigate.

1933 - Merstham Brigade

In addition to the now redundant sub stations at South Park; Meadvale and Earlswood, there also existed a separate Merstham Brigade. This was incorporated into the Borough Brigade in 1933 when the Borough expanded to take in Merstham. It became 'M' division in addition to the existing 'A' and 'B' divisions of Redhill and Reigate.

Above: The Merstham crew pose outside the gates of Merstham House in Quality Street c1933
Below: Merstham cup winners c1935

Notes for Chapter Five

[1] *Surrey Mirror Sept. 9th 1913 article on William Hockett's retirement.*

[2] *The store later became Grime's Picture Pavilion, generally known as 'The Pavilion' and later The Rio Cinema. It was to close after a fire in 1965.*

[3] *Redhill was a very wet area. It had numerous streams flowing through it but most of these have been culverted. It has taken a number of years for the land upon which Redhill was built to dry out. In the 1950s buses and lorries passing down Station Road East towards the railway station would make the ground shake, a phenomenon not noticeable today. Much land once covered in ponds and reeds has dried out or been drained and used for building.*

[4] *This is the last mention of Chief Officer Rouse in the general text. See appendix 2 for more information.*

End of an era - members of the Borough Brigade in the late 1930s, photographed for perhapse the last time before the brass helmet was replaced with the war time model

Chapter Six

The Second World War and After

When war appeared imminent the Government funded the recruitment by local authority fire brigades of auxiliary firemen and women. Many took up full-time service when war was declared whilst others performed part-time duties. Following the severe raiding of this country by the Luftwaffe it became obvious that there was a need for standardisation within the fire service and the Government formed the National Fire Service in 1941, when all brigades were absorbed into one national fire service.

Major Rouse demonstrates to the members of the Colman Institute the process of setting into a hydrant c1937

The Government promised that the service would return to local government control when the emergency was over, but it was not until 1948, three years after the war ended, that this happened, and then it went to County control, not back to the Boroughs as before, although some County Boroughs, such as Croydon, were designated as fire authorities.

The Reigate Fire Brigade prepares for war in 1939

Reigate's Breathing Apparatus competition winners pose with their "Salvus" set

Reigate despatch rider Fred Bridle astride his 650cc Matchless

The recruitment of A.F.S. personnel before the Second World War resulted in around two hundred men eventually being employed in the service locally; quite an advance on the original six. By 1944 many of these were ex-retained men who had considerable service in the Brigade. The longest record was held by Leading Fireman C.V.Winchester (part-time) who had joined in 1905. He was appointed sub-officer in 1913, engineer in 1921, assistant district officer, and later district officer, in 1925. He had also served with the Royal Garrison Artillery 1917-19. He was commended four times for work done at fires in the Borough.

A Dennis 'light 6' driven by Bert Abbott c1940.

A.F.S. personnel outside Reigate Station c1940.

Many others also had considerable service records. Leading Fireman W.G.Charman was attached to the Reigate N.F.S., which was begun in 1941, on a whole-time basis, joined in 1910 and became sub-officer in 1926. He served as a corporal from 1914-19 with the 24th County of London Regiment. In 1928 he was commended for action at an ammonia fire at Reigate.

Section leader H.C.Young had 30 years of service. Assistant sub-officer 1926, sub-officer 1929, he was commended in 1929 by the Reigate Borough Council Watch Committee for meritorious service at a fire at Hillside School, and again in 1938 for service at a fire at Cornwallis, a Reigate private house. At the outbreak of WW2 he joined the A.F.S. on a whole-time basis as acting station officer. He went to Redhill in 1941 and was appointed section leader in 1942. He held the Fire Brigade Association's 15 years service medal with bar for the next 5 years, as well as the Reigate Borough medal for 15 years service. Before his Brigade service began he had, at the age of 19, joined the Queen's Royal Regiment, attaining the rank of sergeant in 1914 and completing 5 years service in Mesopotamia and India. He was the holder of the 1914-15 Star, the Victory and General Service medals.

In addition to these men there were others who, during WW2, had seen various terms of Fire Brigade and First World War military service. Fireman J.A.Browning, a part-timer at Reigate had 24 years service; Fireman D.Green, a whole-time N.F.S man in the 1940s had joined in 1921; Fireman A.P.Meakin had been with the Middlesex Regiment for 12 years before joining the whole-time service in 1923; part-timer W.Mitchell saw service in the Queen's Royal West Surrey Regiment during the Great War and joined the Brigade in 1927; A.E.G.Martin, divisional fire prevention officer at Betchworth, joined the Reigate Brigade in 1928, became ambulance officer and assistant sub-officer in 1930, sub-officer in 1934, and station officer in 1937; whole-time firemen A.E.Dean and G.E.Finch each had 15 years' service; Company Officer M.V.Byrne, Officer-in-Charge of Reigate Station, an Irish Guardsman 1917-22, joined in 1933, became assistant sub-officer in 1939, sub-officer the same year, and was also commended for action at the Cornwallis fire. 'Paddy' Byrne went on post war with the Surrey Fire Brigade as station officer in charge of Leatherhead fire station, and then Walton-on-Thames fire station before retiring.

1939 - South Park Fire Station

One new fireman was George Lucas who joined the A.F.S. in March/April 1939 at South Park. The station was situated in the premises of Ernest Crust, a wheelwright and carriage builder of Allingham Road, part of his building being taken over for the duration with Mr Crust continuing business as normal in the remainder of the works. There is a link here with earlier parts of this history, for Ernest Crust had himself been in the fire service in previous years, as has his father, Martin Crust, before him. The business had previously belonged to his father who, much earlier in the century, had rented premises in Priory Road for the stationing of the fire appliance before it was moved to other premises close to the Holmesdale pub. Also, working for Ernie Crust was Robert (Bob) Woodhouse, another ex-fireman from the earlier part of the century.

The station housed a commandeered lorry for carrying equipment and towing a pump. Lorries belonging to the East Surrey Water Company and to Surrey Value Timber Company had been commandeered and one was used at Reigate while the other was used at South Park. There was no telephone in the station and during the day messages were relayed from the call box in the post office across the road. At night someone had to be situated in the post office to take messages. There were two shifts, a twelve-hour day shift and a twelve-hour night shift, and before either went off duty it had to turn out the vehicle and tour the area being covered, which was all of South Park, to ensure there were no fires. This was a procedure whose origins may have originally been set in a kind of logic but the firemen of the time saw little sense in it. Someone in authority must have

General purpose lorry

eventually agreed with them as the procedure was later dispensed with.

Part of the front of the station building was sandbagged as protection against bomb blast, as were most public buildings. If the words 'Fire Station' appeared anywhere it was certainly not above the main door, as that position was occupied by a number of statements concerning its associations, including 'The Reichstag', 'Mein Kampf' and 'The Dawn Patrol', all painted with some skill (but not quite that with which Ernie Crust painted his coach lines).

Fireman George Lucas had been on holiday at Weymouth when news of the imminent declaration of war was given. He returned on the actual day of declaration to find that had he returned the day before he would have received the rank of Leading Fireman, but as he was one day late had missed out. He went on permanent night shift, and in his time of just over a year of duty at South Park had no calls via at the post office telephone and no fires. Other men stationed at South Park in the early years of the war included Alf Williams, Ernie Apps, Mike Hyde (or Hide) the driver, and Bill Jordan.

Bombing had been expected to commence very soon after declaration of war but did not happen immediately. This short period of unexpected calm was known as the 'phoney war', and because of the lack of enemy action on the home front at that time some firemen were stood down. George Lucas was one of these, and recalled that there was bad feeling caused because there were junior men that he had helped train who continued in service. Nevertheless his service ceased in December 1940 and he had to find other employment. Opportunity duly arrived and in the January of 1941 he went to be an army driver for the Colonel of the Merstham RHQ of the 43rd Light Ack-Ack Regiment. This he did until 1942/3 when he went on a mechanics course and took up that occupation in the army until his demob in January 1946.

Back in civvy street George joined his brother's taxi service. Within a month the old Allingham

Above & below - Redhill N.F.S. c1942

From the painting "London Fireman" by Paul Dessau, exhibited in the Royal Academy, 1944

Craven 'A'
FOR YOUR THROAT'S SAKE
10 FOR 1'2 • 20 FOR 2'4
CARRERAS • 150 YEARS REPUTATION FOR QUALITY

Road premises of Ernie Crust, once the South Park A.F.S. fire station, came up for sale. Ernie was keen to retire and George and his brother bought the premises and started a garage there, South Park Motors, which ran for a great many years until George himself retired. The garage was still there in 1997 with the same name but different ownership.

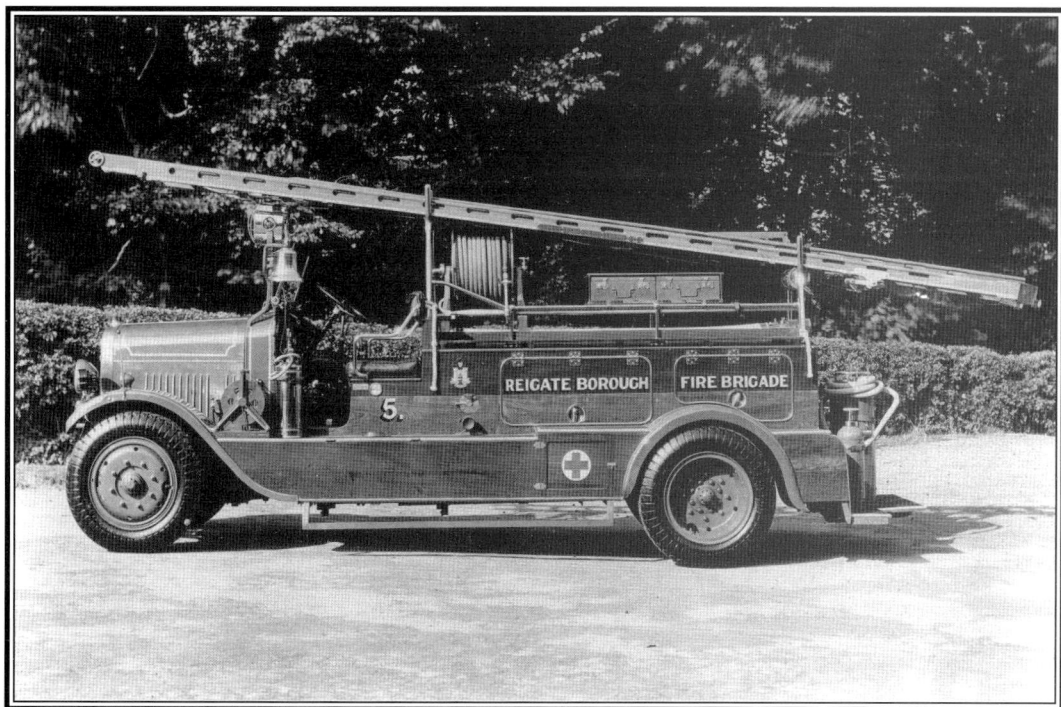

Reigate's second pump (water tender ladder) c1938

1942 - Merstham Fire Station

Les Warne served as an A.F.S. part-timer at 32 Fire Force at Merstham from 1943-44. His duties were two twelve-hour night shifts at the station in Station Approach North, shared with an Officer-in-Charge, a duty man and four or five others. It was a duty for which he received little or no pay and carried out because he was told he had to. He later found out that as he was a student, A.F.S. duties were not necessary after all.

The only full-time personnel Les was aware of was the OIC, a sub-officer whose name was Batters and who lived in Brook Road. Equipment consisted of a tender with a ladder, not an escape, and a pump pulled behind an Austin towing vehicle. The pumps were tested on Sundays, when the firemen would meet at the reservoir - otherwise known as M.A.Ray's pit behind the church that then stood on the corner of Nutfield and Bourne Roads.

Unlike the South Park station of a couple of years before, the telephone was laid on directly into the station. It rang far more often on calls testing the line than it ever did on actual fire calls. In his time there he only experienced one fire, and that was not caused by enemy action. Les remembers that the siren at Merstham was sited on top of a tall pole in the council yard by the railway bridge in Nutfield Road.

1943 - Woodhatch Fire Station

Woodhatch station was situated at the foot of Cockshot Hill on the opposite side of the road to the Angel public house. On a piece of ground now partly occupied by a Catholic church were two houses, the larger of which was occupied by around twenty men on a 24 hour on, 24 hour off rota. They were not there as a local force but as an A.F.S. pool under the control of Reigate Station and capable of turning out at short notice in order to fight fires almost anywhere.

Borough personnel c1940

Test runs would see them turned out and sent as far as the south coast. Some of these, in the winter of 1943/44, were in extreme conditions of fog and bitter cold. They would travel with a number of men in a convoy of several vehicles. The water tender, driven by Ted Moore, would be in front followed by the towing vehicle driven by Jock McCutcheon, the latter vehicle with ladder and men inside and pump behind. Because of the conditions no test run's destination was reached that winter. On one occasion the towing vehicle broke down at Washington. A long wait of several hours in the bitter cold was followed by more hours in even more bitter cold when the rescue vehicle sent was the escape, and men had to sit outside for the whole of the return journey with just a blanket around them. Back at Woodhatch several of those on the side of the escape were so cold they had to be lifted off.

Another time the vehicles failed to arrive at their destination was when the towing vehicle ran into the back of the tender in fog. This was not on a test but on a run to Portsmouth to deal with fires resulting from enemy action. The blitz on Portsmouth was an ongoing affair and firemen were sent from all over the south of England to spend a fortnight in Portsmouth to deal with the effects. Off duty men were allowed into the cinemas free as long as they were in uniform.

Woodhatch was full of incident. The CO was like a Station Officer, although probably not of that rank. In 1943/44 it was Mr Knight who either still was, or more probably had been, manager of

N.F.S. Personnel line up for Home Office inspection, at the rear of Reigate fire station c1944

Reigate N.F.S. full turnout

Martin Dunsford's men's tailoring shop in Reigate. One night he went out for a drink to the Angel pub with his 2nd in command, leaving a fireman on guard at the entrance to the station with a double-barrelled shotgun. What there was to be guarded is uncertain, and it was certainly felt by some at the time that arming firemen was a little extreme. It was a one off event, however, as on their return the two men were treated to the effects of both barrels by their own guard. The shotgun was thereafter dispensed with.

It was the time when officers were split from their men by the union, or at least by the threat of it, and several of the Woodhatch men had been transferred there because of their outspoken views on the subject. Whether it was the union, the men, or the attitude of those men towards the times in general, is unclear, but behaviour is reported to have at times fallen below that normally expected at fire stations.

1948-1957 - St. David's

With the 1948 denationalisation of the N.F.S and the reversion of fire brigades to county control, most counties were able to simply take over the existing control structure as it was. Surrey's situation was different because it suffered from the problem that its brigades had been subject to control from two regional HQs and three Fire Force HQs, with the consequence that there was no single centralised HQ for Surrey to organise its brigades from. It sought to rectify this problem, and it was in 1952 when the idea of setting up this new HQ at St. David's at Reigate was first aired publicly. Incorporated in the scheme was a plan to replace the stations at Redhill and Reigate with a single station. The following year the idea was given substance by the Minister of Housing and Local Government when he announced that he had approved the purchase of the property.

There was opposition to the idea and a public enquiry on July 19th, 1953, prior to the ministerial announcement. The building proposed to see new use as a Fire Brigade HQ had previously been

Above: Dennis F12's turn out at St David's c1958
Below: Dennis F24's line up at St David's c1960

Recruits are put through their paces with hook ladders and lowering lines at the HQ site Reigate c1965

Live carry down on the wooden bailey escape ladde, while branch men control the back pressure of an a type branch c1974

used as a preparatory school and then the home of Spurgeon's Orphanage before becoming vacant early in 1953. Opposition centred on the fact that there would be interference with the character of the area, that the scheme would be costly, and that the premises would be better used as a school and the grounds as an open space. These arguments did not carry the day, however.

A problem concerning the chapel attached to the ex-school arose. Existing pews, choir stalls, stained glass windows (one a memorial to ex-boys who had fallen in the South African war) some of which were gifts and dedicated to former pupils, could not be simply removed and destroyed, yet with them in situ the building was of no use to the Fire Brigade. The problem was solved when the Diocese of Southwark agreed to remove all these relics at their own expense for installation as required in alternative churches. A difficult problem had been solved, for although none of these items were consecrated it was good to know that no desecration would take place.

St. David's became operational as the Surrey Fire Brigade HQ in October 1955, with Redhill and Reigate fire stations closing at their respective sites and combining at St. David's. When opened the new HQ provided local fire cover, plotted the amount of equipment available for use anywhere in the county, and also provided a tactical training centre where preparation for the kind of fires that may be caused in an atomic war was carried out. This last was a Home Office operation that was termed a mobile fire column that moved elsewhere in 1964.

Post war A.F.S crews train with their Green Goddess fire appliances, part of the mobile fire column based at St. David's Reigate c 1960

Appendix I
Fires in the Borough

It has been said that a fire is a fire, presumably meaning that from a historical point of view there is little that can be said about one fire that cannot be said about all of them. But all unintentional fires are terrible things. With destruction of property and sometimes loss of life they are significant events that are unlikely to be forgotten by those who experience them. They become part of the history of an area and therefore have a place in records of that history. So although this book is about the Fire Brigade itself, it does seem incomplete to ignore some of the more notable reasons for its existence. It was therefore decided to record details of all fires noted in research, and although far from complete, the list is included here. Where an address only is given no more details are available.

1835
Reigate Heath -Two cottages destroyed and a child burnt to death
1866
Station Road, Redhill
1867
Mr Otto's
Nash's farm
1868
Lesbourne Lands
Mr Brown's at Redhill
1869
Mead's, Wray Park, Reigate
1871
Mr Pullen's, Lesbourne Lands
Temperance Hotel, near Reigate Station
Nutley Lane, Reigate - both Brigades attended
1872
Kingswood
1873
Colley Farm, Reigate
White Hart, Reigate
1874
Philanthropic Farm School, Redhill
1877
New Pond Farm, Redhill
High Street, Reigate
1878
June 27th - *Mr John Harrison's Bridlecomb Farm, Buckland.* Three large barns, tools, crops and stored threshed wheat destroyed.
1879
Dr Lloyd's on Christmas Day

1880
Mrs Milexes?
Birkheads Road, Reigate
Bell Street, Reigate
1882
Linkfield Lane, Redhill
Mr Gurney's
Mercer's Farm, Merstham
Market Place (Reigate or Redhill?)
1883
Mr Gordon's in Bell Street, Reigate
1884
Ivy House Farm, Bletchingley
Brighton Road, Redhill
Alderstead
Mr Alexander's at Woodhatch
West Street
Buckland
Rev. H.Goss's, Redhill
Mr Lillyman's, Redhill
Fountain beer house, Redhill
London Farm, Horley
Mill Street, Redhill
1885
Mr Collyer's, Buckland
Whitehall Farm. South Park
Mr Tomlinson's, Bell Street, Reigate
Crutchfield Farm, Hooley
Merstham
Isbells, Cockshot Hill, Reigate - one of Reigate's oldest dwellings, with two windmills beside it and a history going back to the fourteenth century, was destroyed. William Wix shown as living there in 1868
1886
Colley Farm
Buckland
Fire at or near Red Lion Inn, Dorking Road. Both Brigades (plus Dorking?)
Petridge Wood
Stenning's timber yard, Brighton Road, Redhill.
1887
Salfords Mill, Horley
Mr Mead's in Market Place (Reigate or Redhill?)
1888
Linkfield Street
Ladbroke Road, Redhill - Mr H.R.Charlwood commended for averting gas explosion.
Cockshot Hill, Reigate
Linkfield Lane, Redhill

1889
Mark Street, Reigate
Warwick Road, Redhill
Cotlands Farm, Charlwood
1890
Grove Road, Redhill
Home Cottage Inn, Cavendish Road, Redhill
Burrell's Farm
Reigate Hill
Quaker's Meeting House, Reigate
William Stenning and Son
Harewood, South Park, Bletchingley
Mr King's, near Frenches, Redhill
Redstone
Mr Grimes', Redhill
Cage Yard, Reigate
Mr Simpson's, Wray Park, Reigate
Near Wiggie, Redhill
White Hart Tap, Reigate
Queen's Arms Inn, Redhill
1891
Battlebridge, Merstham
Staplehurst Farm
Near Nutley Lane, Reigate
London Road, Redhill
Ladbroke Road., Redhill
Hathersham Farm, Nutfield
Reigate Heath.
Gloucester Road, Redhill
London Road, Redhill
1892
Hatchlands Road, Redhill
1893
Bell Street, Reigate
Rear of Reigate High Street
Moors Place Farm
Brewer Street Farm, Bletchingley
1894
Earlswood
Reigate Heath
Merstham
Colley Farm, Reigate
Mill Street, Redhill
Garlands Road, Redhill
Woodhatch, Reigate, property of John Clutton
Hartswood, Reigate
Clay Hall Farm

7th November - *Grammar School, Reigate*

1895

March 19th - *Bee Hive Beer House, Dovers Green* - Two part boarded and brick built houses, one used as branch post office, the other as a beer house, well alight with roof falling in when Fire Brigade arrived. Fire was caused by Mrs Burberry ascending stairs with paraffin lamp after taking letters to post office. She caught her foot in stair carpet and fell. Paraffin spilt and ignited house.

March 25th - *White House, West Street.* This was a chimney fire that looked worse due to build up of heat and smoke. Of 25 pails of water put down the chimney very little reached the room so little damage was done to premises by smoke or water. House the home of Mr Pollen.

April 14th and 15th - *The Moors, Reigate Heath.* Hay Stack.

Upper Bridge Road. Redhill

The Steam Laundry, Redhill

1896

January 13th - *Farm near Betchworth Station.* Brigade arrived to find farm building, its contents, plus one retriever dog, well alight.

January 12th - *Mount Field, Meadvale.* Kitchen of building called Mount Field alight.

April 21st - *5 Allingham Road, South. Park, Reigate.* Chimney fire.

July 6th - *Laurence's Farm, near Buckland.* Farm buildings and 4 stacks alight.

Betchworth

Brighton Road

Linkfield Lane

Nutfield

Alderstead Farm

Ford Bridge Farm, Merstham, property of Jeremiah Colman

Old Garlands, Redhill

November 2nd - *Hook Farm, Leigh*, Property of Duke of Norfolk. 2 Stacks.

1897

March 21st - *13 Smith Road, South Park.* This chimney fire was dealt by the local South Park Brigade members of M.Crust, E.Crust and R.Woodhouse.

June 14th - *Pitt's Furniture Repository, Warren Road, Reigate.* This was a considerable fire. The Reigate Brigade arrived first and were hampered by a water plug bursting and had to go further afield for a water supply. The Redhill and Dorking Brigades also attended, followed later by the Horley Brigade, but they were not required by this time and left. The firemen were also hampered by horses being brought out of an adjacent stables and released in the road, and by a disorderly crowd which the police had to control.

July 4th - *Colley House Farm.* Cart lodge and stable alight and falling in on arrival of Brigade.

Mr Grimes premises

August 17th - *Wraylands, Wray Park, Wray Common.* Redhill Brigade arrived first, Reigate Brigade followed and gave assistance, Dorking Brigade arrived but was not needed. Top story destroyed.

September 27th - *Mr W.Port's Butchers shop, High Street, Reigate.* Butcher's smock left hanging in fireplace caught alight from fire in grate left burning. Damage confined to one room.

November 2nd - *15 South Albert Road, Reigate.* Fire in roof of attached laundry caused by defective copper chimney.

1898

February 3rd - 33, *North Albert Road.* Chimney fire

Earlswood

May 26th - 5, Birkheads Road. Basement fire out when Brigade arrived.

Brighton Road, Redhill

July 28th - *Marriages, Bell Street, Reigate*. Workshop 'built to great height' sustained £3,000-4,000 damage. Two horses saved and large quantity of gunpowder removed. Reigate Brigade attacked fire from High Street while Redhill Brigade attacked fire from rear after approaching via White Hart gardens.

Wiggie, Redhill
Castle Hill Farm, Bletchingley
Churchfelle, Reigate
High Street, Reigate

1899

Cromwell Road, Redhill
Allingham Road, Reigate
The Pear Tree, Nutley Lane, Reigate (a common lodging house)
White Hall Farm, Gatton
Fairlight, South Road, Reigate
Upper Gatton
Mayfield, Wray Park Road., Reigate
Noahs Ark, Redhill
Alniversity ? School

September 30th - *Dukes Head, Brockham Green*, alight top to bottom on arrival but Dorking brigade had fire in hand so Reigate returned after resting horses.

October 30th - *40 Nutley Lane*. Premises had only that day opened as a hairdressers, unprotected lamp had fired ceiling. Fire quickly controlled.

Quarry Barn, Merstham

November 14th - *Castle Field, haystack*.

1900

Near Redhill station
Masons Bridge Farm

June 11th - *41 Somers Road*. Attic fire. Small sleeping child, Annie Smith, saved from upper bedroom by servant Miss Naomi Smith. House owned by Mr Pilleau who was away.

Nutfield Court

August 15th

Shalford Mill burnt out 2nd time.
Dancy and Goodman, Redhill
Linkfield Corner
Isolation Hospital

1901

16 Earlsbrook Road
107 Cromwell Road
Monson Road
29 Nutley Lane

February 9th - *Mr J.T.Peat's, Bell Street. Reigate* A back bedroom was burnt out. Although the Fire Brigade arrived promptly two of their number were not called, an omission that had Fred Legg writing in his report that electric bells ought to be considered for use once the new station at Reigate was brought into use.

March 8th - *Old Isolation Hospital* ablaze and partially collapsed. Reigate Brigade turned out but returned as Redhill Brigade was dealing and Reigate's services would be to no avail. Reigate

The fire at Nicol's store, Station Road, Redhill May 27th 1901. More details of this fire appear in 'A History of Redhill' Volume Two, by Alan Moore

Brigade encountered a thunderstorm on way back and all gear soaked and had to be thoroughly cleaned and dried.

May 27th - *Nicol's drapery store in the Market Square, Redhill*, was totally destroyed. This was the Borough's most well known and it's worst fire.

July 11th - *Grammar School, Reigate*. Fire in chemical laboratory.

Mr Smith's Studios, Redhill. Circumstances surrounding this fire were brought up in Council after a Mr Sanders reported that he had raised the alarm by going in person to the police station but that the police had sent a man to see whether the Fire Brigade was needed before a policeman was sent to call each of the Redhill fireman. Mr Sanders thought that this delay was unnecessary but was told that this was the rule. He said that the whole system needed review and that electric bells were needed to call the Fire Brigade. The Mayor remarked that his report on the fire appliances had been before the Watch Committee for four months but no action had been taken (presumably this report included the use of bells) and it was now understood that early action *would* be taken. (Source - Newspaper article in Fred Legg's report book) Despite this assurance there is no mention of the matter in Watch Committee minutes until September of 1902, when a single entry states: *'Firemen's houses to be connected to two stations by electric bells.'*

1902

March 20th - *C.B.Roberts and Co., joinery works, Monson Road, Redhill*. Reigate and Redhill Brigades were called to this fire but the whole of the joinery works, machinery and stables, as well as those stacks of timber unable to be saved, was destroyed. The adjacent properties of South View in London Road and other close properties received minor damage.

April 5th - *29 Nutley Lane*. A cripple fell asleep on sofa whilst smoking. Minor damage dealt with by Fireman Dean who lived nearby, and Fireman Whitmore.

May 24th - *41 & 43 High Street, Reigate*. Fire, possibly caused by gas ring left on, burned through first floor kitchen, second floor bedroom and into roof. Member of the public asked to call Brigade called Redhill by telephone instead of Reigate, but Reigate eventually called by other members of public. Redhill and Reigate Brigades both fought the fire. Property owned by Mr A.B.Apted.

June 1st - *Stack Yard, Gate Fields, Woodhatch*. Hay stack fire.

September 29th - *13 High Street, Reigate*, Frank Weller, local fire agent for the County Fire Office. Basement gas ring overheated laths in basement ceiling in spite of being protected by iron plate. £1.10.0 damage covered by insurance.

October 15th - *Gas Works, Nutley Lane, Reigate*. Spontaneous combustion of purifier.

Station Road, Earlswood

Garlands Road, Redhill

1903

White Bushes Farm

Copyhold Works

May 18th - *Grammar School*. Fire in chemical lab extinguished by PC Gadd. Fireman Dean attended with hose cart and manual engine arrived 10 minutes later.

38 Earlsbrook Road

June 13th - *Priory Farm, Reigate*. Haystack alight.

June 20th - *4 West Street*, occupied by J.P.Goldsack. Fire caused by lace curtains over flame in upstairs kitchen.

September 12th - *Littleton Farm*. Farm sheds and pigsty destroyed. Caused by unknown person lodging in pigsty. This fire caused F.Legg to again ask the Watch Committee for a steamer as there were only five men available to pump the manual engine, his own men having to do some of this work.

October 4th - *9, Reigate Heath*. Occupied by C.Bonney. Fire in front room extinguished by neighbours. Caused by glass paraffin lamp overturned by accident.

November 3rd - *19 South Road, Reigate.* Fire in bedroom of house.

London Road, Redhill

1904

March 2nd - *Brynbella, Reigate Road. (Mrs Cooper).* Fire in landing linen cupboard.

June 30th - *Burtenshaw's coach-building works and the adjacent Castle Inn, Bell Street, Reigate.* Both Redhill and Reigate Brigades attended a fire that destroyed the workshops of the coach-builder plus the greater portion of the stock there. Damage was also done to the Castle Inn and to an adjacent cottage. The fire was dealt with between 6 a.m. and 10 a.m., but return visits had to be made on two subsequent occasions to quell further outbreaks within the smouldering ruins.

Garibaldi Road

August 2nd - *Sandcross Lane, Reigate.* Haystack fire, property of Mr R.P.Evans, possibly in Prices Lane, although Capt. Legg's report states Sandcross Lane.

August 3rd - *Cronks Hill, Meadvale.* Grass fire in field between Belmont and Furzefield Roads

London Road, Reigate

South Nutfield

1905

Grices, Brighton Road, Redhill

Chart Lodge

Frenches

Prince Albert, Horley

June 23rd - *38 Priory Road, South Park* Fire extinguished with bucket of water. Owner of cottage S.Lewer. This fire was the first in Reigate since the fire at Cronks Hill, Meadvale, a space of 10 months

Chipstead

Athanaeum, Redhill

September 23rd - *Dr J.Walter's, Church Street, Reigate.* Shed at rear alight.

October 28th - *Haystack fire at Mr R.P.Evans, Woodhatch.* Situation was probably Prices Lane as hydrant used was opposite Angel Inn. 1200 ft of hose used, so situation well along Prices Lane.

1906

January 17th - *Electric Light Station.* Pumping out of flooded boiler room and damming incoming waters causing flood. This is probably the only incident recorded here that was not a fire, and one where the engine would have been used to pump water in the normal way but *out* of somewhere and not onto a fire.

Old Rectory, Bletchingley

20 Grove Road, Redhill

January 20th - *Beaufort Road, Reigate.* Motor car alight, cause put down to back firing.

January 25th - *London Road, Reigate.* Chimney fire.

Leysfield Farm, Chipstead

31 North Street, Redhill

February 17th - *Priory House, Reigate.* Chimney fire.

February 20th - *Chart Fields, Reigate.* Hayrick fire

33 High Street, Redhill

Rear of Tower Inn, Redhill. PC Dobney was commended for his discovery of this fire and awarded a gratuity of £1.1.0 as a consequence.

Hatchlands Road

October 29th - *R.P.Evans, Esq., Woodhatch.* 12 tons of coal alight in a stoke-hole was dealt with by flooding the stoke-hole. After that the water was pumped out again. The cause of the fire was reported as unknown but it was noted that the coal was stacked against the boiler. R.P.Evans was having fires at the rate of 1 per year.

1 Ladbroke Road

8 Charman Road

Mr Howard Martin's, Nutfield Road

71 Station Road, Redhill

1907

January 1st - *Mr Benson's, Upper Gatton Park.* This fire demonstrates the more common use of the telephone. The call was received by telephone, as were the calls for most fires. The fire engine started out but as Reigate Hill was to be climbed a stop was made in London Road while an extra horse was waited for. At this stop Fred Legg heard that the Redhill engine was also on its way, and as the rule was that there was only supposed to be one engine out of the Borough at any one time Fred Legg rang Mr Benson's. He was told that the fire was out so he returned to the fire station.

January 10th - *Grapes Hotel, Reigate.* Chimney fire dealt with by Fireman Dean, the Resident Fireman.

43 Station Road.

March 1st - *9 & 11 Holmesdale Road, Reigate.* Reigate Brigade arrived and as two houses were burning the Redhill Brigade was also called, but although they arrived in good time the fire was under control by then and they did not have to connect a hose. Instead they helped clear up and then departed. Both buildings burnt out.

July 19th - *13 and 15 High Street, Reigate (Mr Watson's China and Glass shop, and Mr Deane's fancy and stationary goods shop. Next door Mr Allingham's premises)* The notable thing about this fire is that the brewery staff, who discovered the fire, had their own hose pipe and were able to connect up and start to fight the fire before the Fire Brigade arrived. Damage to the rear of both shops. Serious damage to both shops and their stock, slight damage to Allingham's by water.

Kentwins, Upper Nutfield

Jersey Dairy, Warwick Road, Redhill

Carlton Road, Redhill

August 17th - *Lawrence Farm, Buckland.* Hayrick fire.

Chalmers and Co., Redhill

September 30th - *Noke Farm, Chipstead.* Two oats stacks were alight but there was no water near-by and the nearest hydrant was some way away. Fred Legg laid out 2,200 feet of hose but it was not enough and he had to send back to Reigate for more. This caused considerable delay but the fire was eventually put out and part of the oat stacks saved. 2,670 feet of hose was used in all.

October 5th - *Hill Croft, Smoke Lane, Reigate.* A well-named venue for a chimney fire.

1908

January 8th - *More Place, Betchworth.* Nine haystacks at More Place Farm alight. Reigate Brigade only got to baths entrance when they were told that Betchworth Brigade had put fires out.

February 13th - *8 Howard Road, Reigate.* Chimney fire.

February 28th - *Mr J.W.B.Northover, Bell Street., Reigate.* Shop well alight. Stock insured by Sun Fire Office, of which Mr Northover was the local agent.

March 13th - *Hazlemere, Beaufort Road, Reigate.* Chimney fire.

March 20th - *Ferndale, Warren Road., Reigate.* Chimney fire.

April 5th - *Manor Farm, Kingswood.* Rick fire.

60 Station Road, Redhill

April 28th - *Station Hotel, Kingswood.* Whole of first floor and roof destroyed, ground floor severe water damage. Railway staff connected their own hose to nearest hydrant, Reigate Brigade connected to adjacent hydrant but unable to get water. They connected to another hydrant and got two branches going. They had 13 firemen and 3 assistants. Sutton Water Company connections different pattern to Reigate's but suitable connectors carried. Epsom Brigade arrived but were unable to assist because of no other hydrant available and pond 700 yards away. Sutton Brigade called but failed to turn out.

<u>May 18th</u> - *Rookery Farm, Kingswood.* Granary fire extinguished by local employees.

<u>June 18th</u> - *Whitening factory, The Clears, Reigate.* Factory used for making whitening and prepared distemper alight. Furnaces for drying the whitening overheated and set alight creosoted timber structure forming part of the building designed to create draught. Iron sheet roof fell in but four brick walls left standing. Damage estimated at around £1,000. Machinery consisting of a large gas engine and putty mill was saved.

Fullers Earth

<u>August 5th</u> - *Kemps Farm, Buckland.* Sparks from bonfire set light to 3 cowsheds, 3 sets of stabling, a granary, various other sheds and carriage houses plus a harness room. These were all destroyed but the main farmhouse was saved.

<u>November 7th</u> - *Motor car LN 7740 at Reigate Hill Road.* Fire extinguished by driver. This fire prompted Fred Legg to ask for chemical extinguisher to fight petrol fires.

<u>November 23rd</u> - *9 Warren Road, Reigate.* Lodger removing petrol from motor cycle with lamp burning nearby. Fire put out by men before brigade arrived.

<u>December 26th</u> - *Garthlands, Reigate Heath.* Nursery on 1st floor alight due to joists overheated by flue.

<u>December 28th</u> - *Nutley Hall public house, Nutley Lane, Reigate.* House and stables gutted. Adjoining buildings saved by three jets from neighbouring hydrants. This was one of the more difficult fires as not only did the fire have too good a hold to save the Nutley Hall but there was a severe frost that night and men and hoses were frozen. Two people had to jump from windows but without injury.

1909

<u>January 12th</u> - *94 High Street, Reigate.* Small fire within premises.

<u>January 23rd</u> - *Kemp Farm, Buckland.* Hayrick.

<u>February 7th</u> - *Flanchford Farm, Leigh.* Kitchen chimney with bacon loft alight.

<u>February 9th</u> - *Mr A.B.Apted's premises, 25 Doods Road.* Timber store and carpenters shop ablaze. Adjacent property belonging to Mr O.C.Apted damaged.

<u>March 11th</u> - *Tregwort, Blackborough Road, Reigate.* Chimney fire.

<u>March 31st</u> - *Leith Villa, 42 Reigate Hill, premises occupied by Lord Richard Browne.* Smoke was coming from cracks in chimney, no fire. Premises owned by Mr Curruthers of Croydon Road.

<u>April 6th</u> - *37 Deerings Road, Reigate.* Chimney fire.

<u>April 29th</u> - *Reigate Garage, Bell Street, Reigate.* Car P 2243 alight outside garage. Chemical extinguisher used first then water.

<u>July 1st</u> - *Firlands, Reigate Road, premises of Surgeon General, Robert Rouse.* Rubbish fire extinguished by police. The alarm raised by Capt. Rouse who was about to become Chief Officer of the Borough brigades. [1]

<u>August 11th</u> - *Post Office, Reigate Heath.* Fire in bedroom, out when Brigade arrived.

<u>16th December</u> - *Stoneman's in Cromwell Road, Redhill.* Fire in the early hours occurred in the coffin polishing room. Captain Mason and Chief officer Rouse attended. This fire is notable in as far as it as it seems to have been Chief Officer Rouse's first fire since taking up that post.

1910

Trower's warehouse in St Johns Terrace Road, Earlswood. Hay, straw and Linseed produced a fire that was notable for the amount of manpower that was available to deal with it. Mr Bonwick, the Earlswood Station Master saw smoke coming from the building and rushed across, arriving just as the alarm was already being given by telephone from someone inside. Apart from the alarm giver there was a Mr Welch from the gas company in the building, and he turned off the gas supply from a two inch incoming main. First on the scene was the Earlswood sub-station crew followed by the Redhill crew with their manual engine under Superintendent Mason. Several policemen were at the scene and rendered their aid in various ways while some boys formed a bucket chain at the rear of the building. More boys, this time a squad from the Farm School, arrived with their manual engine. Next on the scene was Captain Rouse, taking command, and he was followed by the Reigate Brigade under Superintendent Legg. The fire was extinguished about an hour after the alarm had been given with about £1,000 worth of insurance covered damage done.

1910

Deerings Road, Reigate
Whitebushes, Redhill
Tar washing machine
'Mount' Training Home, Wray Common, Reigate. Florence Victoria Skelton, a 17 year old inmate, died three weeks after being badly burnt when her dress caught fire while she was warming herself at a fire.

1911

Blanford Road, Reigate
13 Bell Street, Reigate
Market Stores, Reigate
Hillside School
36 Effingham Road, Reigate
23 & 25 Nutley Lane
Pantechnicon on Reigate Hill (see p71)
Hayrick, Batts Hill, Redhill
Reigate Heath
Railway embankment near Reigate Gas Works
Railway embankment rear of Doods Road. Reigate
Crossways Farm, Upper Gatton
Reigate Heath
Rookery Farm
Philanthropic Farm School, Redhill The school owned a manual fire engine (bought from the Reigate Corporation) which was used to attack a fire in a hay stack until the Redhill Brigade arrived. The Warden was so pleased with the discipline, good temper and readiness to work of the boys that he gave the whole school a half day holiday and restored some privileges previously withdrawn for some want of discipline. The person responsible for the fire (referred to as an incendiary) was a old pupil of the school. He was caught by the police and sentenced to 1 year's prison.
Reigate Heath
Grammar School Hill
Margery Farm, Kingswood
Chart View, Reigate Road
21 Brook Cottages
9 Holmesdale Road., Reigate

17 Brighton Road
Reigate Heath (Golf Club liable)
2nd fire at Nicol's, Redhill

1912

24th March - *Tanyard of Messrs Samuel Barrow and Brother (Ltd), in Tanyard Lane, Redhill.* On Monday evening, a few minutes after nine o'clock, the Borough Fire Brigade received a call to a fire at the Tannery. A shed measuring 14' by 12' standing in the yard and detached from other buildings, used as a meal room by the men employed at the tannery, was well alight and before many minutes had elapsed the roof had fallen in. Employees of the tannery and others obtained water by means of buckets, and to a certain extent were able to subdue the flames. Upon the arrival of the Brigade with the horse manual, they quickly secured a hose to a hydrant and within a minute of two the fire had been entirely extinguished. The firemen were under the command of Supt. Mason, and they were quickly upon the scene after receiving the call. The damage was estimated at £50.

Colley Manor
Residence of Coachman J.T.Coombs (He became coachman at HQ of London Salvage Corps)
8 Upper West Street, Reigate
South Park Farm, Bletchingley
Wallfields, West Street
Entrance lodge of Colley House
Ashcombe, Alma Road
118 Station Road, Redhill
London Road, Redhill

Philanthropic School, Redhill - The old pupil of the school, on release from a year in prison for setting fire to a haystack in of the Philanthropic, returned to set fire to two more. Once again the boys rallied to the call (literally, as the fire alarm was a bugle call) and attacked the fire and then assisted the Redhill Brigade when it arrived. The boys were again rewarded and the old pupil was returned to prison, this time with hard labour.

Colgate Farm, Nutfield

1913

3rd Jan - *Foster's Temperance Hotel, Brighton Road, Redhill* was destroyed by fire at the end of the year. The Hotel stood at the top of the Brighton Road near the Cutting. It was a large building which faced Redhill and was well known as a centre for London and Croydon cycling clubs, while locally it was the was the HQ of the Woodlands Social Club and the Woodlands Bowling Club. Originally it had been a private residence but the original building had been greatly added to. The fire started in one of the first floor bedrooms. The alarm was given by Mr and Mrs Foster who, on going outside, met PC Claydon and PS Watson. These two made sure no-one was on the premises and called the Fire Brigade, the call being received at 7.31 p.m. Both the Reigate and Redhill Brigades attended, and the collapse of the roof shortly after their arrival showed the hold that the fire had. The horsed escape and water tower was sent for and subsequently brought from where it was kept at the Reigate fire station and run up to the front of the building and, with other hoses, attacked the fire. By 9.30 the flames were completely doused but newspaper reports noted that had there been an escape and water tower at Redhill, and had they been used this time would have been bettered. It was suggested that a motor turbine escape would have been even better. Four bedrooms were undamaged, four were damaged by water, and nine were destroyed. The ground floor was severely damaged by water. The firemen finally left the scene at 3 a.m. The building and its contents were insured and the damage was assessed at £1,500. The hotel did not re-open.

1 Fengates Road, Redhill

36 & 38 Priory Road, Reigate
Wellersley Cottages, Grove Road, Redhill
Lightning damage at 'Parkwater', Blanford Road, Reigate
62 Cromwell Road, Redhill
Lindsey's Hotel, High Street, Redhill
Mercer's Farm, Merstham
1915
Redhill and Reigate Laundry on Redhill Common destroyed.
Athanaeum printing works, Brighton Road, Redhill. A motorised fire engine had been purchased the previous year and this fire was its first use.

Fire at the Athanaeum printing works Redhill 1915
1917
Munitions train, Redhill station. (see p94)
1922
Stenning's timber yard, Brighton Road, Redhill. Second fire
1926
Reigate Priory
1928
High Trees School, Salfords.
1929
Victoria Road, Redhill A small grocery shop in, was gutted and its elderly owner, Mr Richard Lee, and his wife lost their lives.
1934
Gatton Hall
1939
2 Market Square, Reigate - Electrical Fire
1940
The Chase, Redhill vacant plot grass fire
Redhill Common, gorse
Sewage Works shed

Funeral of Supt Alf Sear 26th October 1931

Gatton Hall fire, home of Sir Jeremiah Colman February 1934

1939-45
Mellersh and Neale Brewery in Reigate - Offices damaged
Church Road, Merstham Three houses alight in due to incendiary bombs following a night raid
Redstone Hill, (top of) Redhill large house.

1952
Bell Inn, Bell Street, Reigate Top floor burnt out.
Rio Cinema, High Street, Redhill. Damage was considerable. The building stood empty from then on until is demolition and redevelopment.

1959
Trower's Granary, Earlswood.
Hieatt printers, High Street, Reigate

1964
Surrey Mirror offices, Ladbroke Road, Redhill.

1973
Greenfilelds, Warwick Road. This was a fire observed by this author. It was set deliberately by demolition men who had only a bulldozer with which to demolish the old nurse's home with and decided to expedite matters with a match. All was going well until some burning timbers fell onto the front lawn near Warwick Road and the demolition foreman decided to use the bulldozer to push them back inside the building, its front wall having been knocked down. He forgot about, or did not know of, the existence of a basement to the building. The floor gave way and the bulldozer fell in. The foreman clambered out and the Fire Brigade was called. On arrival they hitched a tow-wire to the bulldozer and pulled it out. The building was allowed to burn.

1975 (or later)
St Anne's, Redhill. St Anne's had often been used for escape ladder drill by the Redhill Brigade.

198?
Surrey Value timber yard, Brighton Road, Redhill. This author was in Redhill that evening at 7 p.m. and remembers that the town was full of the smoke and smell of burning carried on a wind from the south.

Notes for Apendix I
[1] *This was the last report to be written by Fred Legg as Captain of the Reigate Fire Brigade. He wrote one more report as Superintendent and thereafter his report book is blank, reports presumably written from then on by the new Chief Officer. The timing of this fire seems rather a coincidence.*

Appendix II
The Legg Family of Reigate

Foreman R. Legg 1854

Engineer E. Legg 1857

Supt. F. Legg 1886

Fireman F. Legg 1915

Aux. Fireman G. Legg 1916

Five generations of the Legg family of fire fighters

Notes on the Legg Family of Reigate

Members of the Legg family have been mentioned at various points in this history. They served for five generations in the local brigade, with other members of the family serving in other brigades. The family history of fire fighting is said to go back to before 1857 when Robert Legg, of West Street, Reigate, was a member of the original Reigate Brigade started in 1809. He was appointed Captain (or Foreman) of the Reigate Brigade.

His son, Edwin, was also a Reigate Fireman. He was killed in 1904 in a building site accident in West Street, Reigate. He went to inspect work going on at the White House, Reigate, during the lunch hour and fell from a ladder. In the list of Brigade members on p39 he is shown as 'Edwin Legg Senior (Engineer'. Also on that list is his son, 'Edwin Legg Junior (Fireman)'. He was a baker and probably not in the fire brigade for very long as he subsequently emigrated to Australia where, ironically, he died in a bush fire.

Fred (not Frederick) Legg, and the first of three Fred Leggs, was another son of Edwin Senior. He was originally from 34, West Street but moved in 1904 to 6, Slipshoe Street. He joined the Reigate Brigade in April 1886. He was appointed Sub-Engineer in 1891 and became Captain of the Reigate Brigade in 1894. He later became Superintendent overall of the Reigate and Redhill Brigades, but when in 1909 Captain Rouse took over overall charge of both forces he stood down to be Captain of the Reigate force only. When Chief Officer Rouse was recalled for military service in 1939 Fred Legg took charge of the whole Brigade again. It was this Fred Legg who was involved with the 1917 fire in a munitions train at Redhill station. In 1891 Fred paraded at Crystal Palace with many others who were inspected by Queen Victoria's grandson, Kaiser Wilhelm of Germany. Fed Legg died in 1939 as Deputy Chief Officer of the Reigate Brigade with 53 years service to his credit.

Crystal Palace burnt down in 1936 and one of Fred's sons, George, who had joined the Croydon Brigade, was involved in fighting the fire that reduced that grand structure to ruins. George fought fires in Croydon throughout the second war, retiring from the force in 1955 and starting a new job as works fireman in a large Croydon commercial establishment.

Another of Fred Legg's sons, John, joined the Wimbledon Fire Brigade. He was unfortunately killed in a 1926 motorcycle accident at the top of Reigate Hill while on his way to work.

The second Fred Legg, of Yorke Road, Reigate, also a son of the first Fred Legg, was the author of a the history of the Brigade previously mentioned. He retired as a sub-officer in 1940 after twenty-five years service. He was an amateur artist and sign-writer who could also turn his hand to many other skills.

His son, the third Fred Legg, (Fred Sherrington Legg, to give him his full name, and often referred to as Sherry) started as a drill class entrant in 1935/6. He was 17 then and the correct age for entry was 18, but he was big for his age. He went into the army in 1939, but did not finally sever his Fire Brigade service until 1942, thus ending the succession of Leggs in the Reigate Brigade that had lasted 85 years or more. Fred was also an amateur artist, and was associated with the North Weald Group from its beginnings.

Appendix III
Fire Personnel Names

In the same way as a list of fires was kept during research, so a list of names of men noted as serving in the Borough of Reigate Fire Brigades was kept. It was not started until 1863 had been reached in research, so a number of additional names will be found in the text of chapters dealing with earlier years. The names are listed here in alphabetical order. Names may appear more than once with varying information, such as additional initials, different dates, different events, and many are probably references to the same person, but as this is not proved each research 'find' has been listed separately. (Asterisks against names refer to the Roll of Honour on p93)

Name	Year	Rank	Brigade	Other Information
Anstey, Evans	1903	Fireman	Reigate	
Apps, Ernie	1940	South Park		
Apted, Job Heath	1863	Captain overall, then Captain at Reigate only		Resigned 1875
Armstrong, Fredk	1901	Fireman	Redhill	Appointed in place of H.Rentell (resigned)
Armstrong	1903	Fireman	Redhill	Resigned
Baker E.H.	1910	Fireman	C district	Appointed from reserve
Baker	1913	Fireman		
Bashford, Edward	1910	Fireman		Appointed in place of W.Woodman (resigned)
Bell, Thomas	1911	Fireman		Appointed in place of T.Whitmore (resigned)
Bell T.	1913	Fireman		Appointed in place of Durrant R., (dismissed)
Bennet G.	1894	Messenger boy		
Bish, Michael	1897		Redhill	Resigned
Bray, George	1887	Fireman	Redhill	Appointed in place of Wm. Howell (resigned)
Chalmers, Frank	1895	Callboy		
Chalmers	1912	Fireman		Injured 1912 at Fosters Hotel fire
Chapman C.	1913	Fireman	B district	Lived in Cromwell Rd. transferred to A. Appointed in place of Sears
Charlwood H.W.	1885	Supt	Redhill	
Charlwood H.W.	1892	Captain	Redhill	
Charlwood H.W.	1899	Captain	Redhill	Resigned
Charman W.G.	1910	Fireman	Redhill	Appointed from reserve in place of J.Phillips(resigned)
Charman	1913	Fireman		
Coomes, John	1910	Driver	HQ	
Cooper J.	1901	Fireman	Redhill	Resigned
Cook, Harry	1887	Reserve	Redhill.	
Cosham	1910	Captain	South Nutfield	
Cork A.	1894	Messenger boy		
Colgate, Henry	1898	Fireman	Reigate	Appointed in place of Whitmore (resigned)
Colgate, Henry	1902	Fireman	Reigate	Resigned due to pressure of employment.
Collins, Levi	1866	Supt	Redhill	Gone when Fuller appointed in 1875

Name	Year	Rank	Brigade	Other Information
Crust M.	1870	Fireman	Reigate	
Crust M.	1892	Foreman	Reigate	
Crust M.	1897	Foreman	Reigate	Service extended for 3 years
	(1888	Martin Crust, wheelwright, 78 Priory Road)		
	(1899	Martin Crust, carriage builder Allingham Road & 78 Priory Road)		
Crust M.	1903	Foreman	Reigate	Resigned. (end of 33 years service)

NOTE: Paper in Fred Legg's book states: *Martin Crust joined the brigade 1870, served as a fireman 14 years, promoted foreman 1885, presented with long service medal 1902 after 31 years service, retired from active service and granted honorary membership 1903, result 32 years active service, 44 years membership in brigade.*

Name	Year	Rank	Brigade	Other Information
Crust E.	1896			Working with father on chimney fire at South Park
Crust E.	1897	Fireman	Reigate	Priory Road, wheelwright aged 25. Appointed Dec 25th 1897
Crust E.	1909	Fireman	Reigate	
Crust E.	1910	Fireman		Resigned
Crust E.	1910	Ex-Fireman	Reigate	12 years service

Ernie Crust took over his father's business. He lived in Eastnor Road, liked his beer, painted coach lines on carriage-work freehand with a paintbrush with very long hairs with great accuracy. (Source Jack Lucas)

Name	Year	Rank	Brigade	Other Information
Dean, William Henry	1895		Reigate	Appointed Reserve Fireman 15th July
Dean W.	1897	Fireman	Reigate	Appointed 1897
Dean W.H.	1902	Fireman	Reigate	June 30th Appointed Resident Fireman at new fire station at £1/week plus rooms, fire and light. Wife to be searcher at 1/6d per duty.
Dean W.	1910	Station Officer	Reigate	(15 years service)
Dean W.	1913	Station Officer	Reigate	Resigned. Promoted Chief Officer of Sutton Coldfield Brigade 1913
Durbridge R.B.	1911	Fireman	A district.	Appointed from reserve
Durrant	1909	Fireman		Appointed from reserve
Durrant	1910	Fireman		
Durrant	1910	Fireman		
Durrant R.	1913	Fireman	South Park	Dismissed
Easton E.	1909	Fireman	Reigate	
Easton W.m.	1910	Fireman		Appointed in place of CA Watson resigned.
Evans Anstey	1909	Fireman	Reigate	Appointed 1903, scaffolder 63 Nutley Lane
Evans A.	1909	Fireman	Reigate	
Evans	1910	Fireman		
Finch, Thomas	1897		Redhill	Lived at 65 Cromwell Road, placed on reserve 23rd Aug
Finch T.	1909	Fireman	Redhill	
Finch T.	1910	Sub-Engineer	Reigate.	(10 years service 1901)
Finch T.	1913	Sub-Engineer		Promoted Engineer in place A. Whitmore
F.Fuller	1875		Reigate	Promoted from Foreman to Superintendent
F.Fuller	1877	Capt.	Reigate	
F.Fuller	1892	Capt.	Reigate	
Handscomb W.J.	11/10/1897	Redhill		
Handscomb W.J.	1900		Redhill	Resigned 23rd May
Gadd George	1902			Appointed in place of Henry Colgate (resigned)

Name	Year	Rank	Brigade	Other Information
Gadd	1903		Reigate	Resigned as appointed stoker at Earlswood Asylum - too far away to continue as brigade member
Green J	1901			Redhill - Appointed in place of G. Rogers (resigned)
Green J.	1911	Foreman		Retired aged 50 in 1913 12 years service
Green, Newton	1/10/1897		Redhill	Appointed London Road Redhill
Green, Newton	1902/3		Redhill	Resigned
Green J	1913			Asked to resign (age limit) 12 years service
Hockett, Gilbert	1907	Fireman	Redhill	Appointed
Hockett Wm.	1897	Sub-Engnr	Redhill	Promoted Engineer

Surrey Mirror Sept 9th 1913

Fireman Hockett joined Redhill Fire Brigade 6th March 1875 - Became foreman 1899. full stop Attended over 200 fires - largest were Nicol's and Quarry Farm barn, lives lost at both. Retired 1913 - Had been treasurer and at retirement retains the job.
Redhill Fire Brigade then had 8 men, and Chief Officer was the late Capt Collins. He served under Capts Vosper, Charlwood, T.Sanders, Mason and C/Officer Rouse. In 1875 fire station was where Chalmers' showroom now (1913) is, then it moved to the Market Field. Subsequently moved to present site (Market Hall) where it's been for 26 years (1887-1913). The manual engine in use is same one as when he started.

Name	Year	Rank	Brigade	Other Information
Hockett W.m.	18/12/1899	Sub-Engnr	Redhill	Promoted Foreman
Hockett W.	1910	Foreman.	Reigate	Retired 1913 aged 50, 38 years service, became hon. Brigade member
Humphrew A.W.		Fireman	Reigaate	Honorary membership 8 years service
Howell W.	1887	Fireman	Redhill	Called upon to resign
Hyde (or Hide), Mike	1940			South Park
James E.J.	1913	Fireman	Earlswood	Appointed from reserve

Jeal, Wm.   Letter of application dated 10-08-1909

Dear Sir, I beg to apply for post of reserve fireman in the Reigate brigade. I am a shopkeeper, and have had several years in building trade. Trusting you will receive my application favourably I remain yours respectfully, William Jeal.

Name	Year	Rank	Brigade	Other Information
Jeal	1910	Fireman		(under 12 months service)
Jennings A.	1903	Fireman	Redhill	Resigned
Jennings C.	1903	Fireman	Redhill	Appointed in place of Jennings A
Jennings F.	1901	Fireman	Redhill	Appointed in place of J.Cooper
Jordan, Bill	1940			South Park
Johnson, Arthur		Fireman	Reigate	Town chimney sweep lived in Slipshoe Street Reigate
Laker J.	1910	Fireman		Committed suicide 1911 (see article about him under section about Ins. Agents)
Lay W.m.	1887	Messenger		
Legg, Edwin	1856	Fireman	Reigate	Appointed
Legg, Edwin	1893		Reigate	Applied for Reigate Captaincy
Legg, Edwin	1897	Engineer	Reigate	Service extended for 3 years
Legg, Edwin	1903	Engineer	Reigate	Resigned (end of 47 years service)
Legg, Fred	1886			Joined Brigade April
Legg, Fred	1891			Appointed Sub-engineer September
Legg, Fred	1894	Sub-Engr	Reigate	Promoted to Captain, March
Legg, Fred	1910	Supt	Reigate	(20 years service in 1910)
Lloyd W.	1903	?	Reigate	Silver medal for 15 years service
Lloyd W.	1909	?	Reigate	Retired by age - made Hon. Fireman
Lockhart S.S.	1910	Captain	Merstham	
Longhurst, Mark	1892	Reserve Fireman		
Lucas, George	1939-40	Fireman	South Park	
Mackrell F.	1897	Fireman	Reigate	Gardener aged 35 of 53 Nutley Lane. Appointed Dec 25th 1897

Name	Year	Rank	Brigade	Other Information
Mackrell	1908	Fireman	Reigate	Resigned
Mackrell F.	1910	Ex-Fireman	Reigate	(10 years service 1910)
Mackrell Frdk Rchd	1909	Fireman	Reigate	Appointed in place J.Muggeridge, res.
Mackrell F.	1912	Fireman	A dist	Resigned?
Mason, John	1897	Engr	Redhill	Promoted Foreman
Mason, John	1899	Foreman	Redhill	Promoted Captain
Mason J.	1910	Supt	Redhill	(30 years service)
Muggeridge F.E.J.	1907	Fireman	Reigate	Appointed
Muggeridge J.	1907	Fireman	Reigate	Moved from Bell Street to Nutley Lane
Muggeridge J.	1908	Fireman	Redhill	Resigned
Miles T.	1903	Fireman	Redhill	Appointed
Perring George	1887	Messenger		
Peskett W.	1909	Fireman	Redhill	
Peskett W.	11/10/97		Redhill	Appointed
Peskett W.H.	1910			Resigned
Peskett W.H.	1910	Ex-Firemen	Redhill	12 years service
Philip, Brian,	1898	Fireman	Reigate	Appointed Oct. 1898
Phillips J.	1910	Fireman	A dist	Appointed in place of Prince
Phillips	1913	Fireman		
Piggot, Charles	1909	Fireman		Appointed from reserve
Piggettt	1913	Sub-officer	Redhill	
Powell W.	1894	Fireman	Reigate	
Powell W.	1909	Fireman	Reigate	
Powell	1910	Fireman		Appointed Sub-Engineer
Powell W.G	1911	Sub-engr		20 years service
Prime, Philip	1897	Fireman	Reigate	Appointed 1897 - 54, Nutley Lane
Prince, Philip	1898	Fireman	Reigate	Appointed aged 24, photographer
Prince P.I.	1910	Ex-fireman	Reigate	(10 years service 1910)

Retired aged about 36 due to ill health and died in 1912 aged 38. Had 11 years service in the Brigade overall. Lived at 54 Nutley Lane, Reigate. Left a widow and two children. His father, Mr Philip C.Prince, B.A., of Oxford, had died only the previous Saturday.

Name	Year	Rank	Brigade	Other Information
Rentell H.	1900	????	Reigate	
Roberts A.C.	1903	Fireman	Redhill	Appointed in place Newton Green
Roberts W.	1903	Fireman	Redhill	Prom Sub-Engineer
Roberts	1907	Fireman	Reigate	Resigned
Roberts	1909	Sub-Engineer		Retired by age - made Hon Fireman
Robinson J	1909	Ex-Fireman	Reigate	Retired by age - made Hon Fireman
Robinson J	1910	Ex-Fireman	Reigate	(20 years service 1910)
Rogers G	1901	Fireman	Redhill	Resigned
Rouse, Major	1909-1941	Chief Officer.		*Major Rouse has numerous mentions in the general text of*

this history but it is not known with certainty when his service ended. It began in Reigate Borough in 1909 and probably finished with the formation of the Nation Fire Service in 1941. There was a presentation to him by the National Fire Brigades' Association at Holborn of the 'Service Rendered' decoration at which was present Mr H.J.Hamblen who was the Mayor of Reigate 1937-41, so his retirement would seem to fall within these dates.

Name	Year	Rank	Brigade	Other Information
Sandill, Henry	1894		Reigate	Appointed to reserve
Saunders, John	1894	Callboy		
Saunders, Thomas	1897	Foreman	Redhill	Resigned
Sears	1910	Fireman	B dist	Appointed from reserve
Sear A.C.	1913	Fireman	B dist	Appointed re fireman HQ @ 25/- wk
Sergent W.	1903	Fireman	Redhill	Appointed. Lived at 103 Earlsbrook Rd.
Sergant W.J.	1907	Fireman	Redhill	Resigned
Sergant T.	1913	Fireman	E dist	Resigned (age limit)
Smith, Frank	1897	fireman	Reigate	Appointed 1897, aged 34, bricklayers labourer of 30 York Rd
Smith F.	May 1910	Fireman		Resigned
Smith F.	1910	Ex-fireman	Reigate	10 years service 1910
*Smith W.H	1917	Ambulance Driver	Reigate	Killed in aaction buried Winereux Cemetary Pas De Calais France

Name	Year	Rank	Brigade	Other Information
Tickner, George	1909	Fireman	Redhill	Appointed in place of F.Mackrell res.aged 25, painter 10 Ledbury Road, Reigate
Tickner	1913	Fireman		
Topliss	1910	Fireman	B Dist	Taken on from reserve
Topliss	1912	Fireman	Redhill	Injured at Fosters Hotel fire
Vosper	1877	Capt.	Reigate	
Walker W.m.	1901	Fireman	Earlswood	Resigned - left area
Walker F.T.	1910	Fireman	C Dist	Appointed from reserve
Ware, Henry Wm	1903	Fireman	Reigate	aged 30, married, of Beaufort Road, Appointed in place of Gadd (resigned)
Ware	1907	Fireman	Reigate	Report on his death
Ware A.J.	1912	Fireman	C dist	Appointed in place C.Bashford resigned
Watson Chas Alfred	1897		Redhill	83 Grovehill Road. Placed on reserve.
Watson C.T.	18/12/1899		Redhill	Appointed
Watson C.T.	1910	Fireman		12 years service
Watson C.A.	May 1910	Fireman		Resigned
Wells, William	1892	Resident Fireman at Reigate		
Wells, William	1894	Fireman	Reigate	Appointed
Wells W.J.	1897	Fireman	Reigate	Resigned due to ill health
Whitmore, Arthur	1897		Redhill	5 CambridgeTerrace - Put on reserve
Whitmore A.	1909	Fireman	Redhill	
Whitmore A.	1910	Engineer	Reigate	10 years service
Whitmore A.	1913	Engineer	Reigate	Promoted Foreman in place of Hockett
Whitmore C.A.	1913	Fireman	Reigate	(47 Nutley La) app. for T Mackrell (res)
Whitmore M.	1894	Fireman	Reigate	
Whitmore M.	1903	Fireman	Reigate	Promoted Engineer (missed 1 step)
Whitmore M.E.	1910	Engineer		Promoted to Foreman
Whitmore M.E.	1911	District Officer		Honorary membership 34 years service
Whitmore T.	1894	Fireman	Reigate	
Whitmore T.	1898	Fireman	Reigate	Asked to resign Aug 1898. 'A most unsatisactory fireman' who had not attended a drill since Feb.
Willett	1910	Fireman	Earlswood	Appointed from reserve
Willett	1913	Fireman		
Williams, Alf,	1940		South Park	
Winchester, Chas	1897		Redhill	Promoted Sub-Engineer
Winchester, Chas	18/12/1899		Redhill	Promoted Engineer
Winchester C.	1907	Fireman	Redhill	Appointed
Winchester C.	1909	Fireman	Redhill	
Winchester C.	1913	Fireman	Redhill	
Winchester C.	1913	Fireman	B dist	Promoted Sub-Officer in place of T. Finch (who had been prom Engineer)
Winchester, Fred Lewis	1911			Appointed to reserve
Winchester, F.L.	1912	Fireman	B dist	Promoted from reserve
Winchester F.	1913	Fireman		
Winchester C	1903	Engineer	Redhill	Deceased
Wood, Charles Thos	1892		Reigate	Promoted Sub-Engineer
Wood	1910	Fireman		
Wood C.	1910	Foreman	Reigate	(20 years service)
Wood C.	1903	Sub-engr	Reigate	Promoted Engineer in place of M Crust (resigned)
Wood C.T	1910	Foreman	Reigate	Retired after 23 years service
Wood W.	1894	Fireman	Reigate	
Wood W.	1903	Fireman	Reigate	Promoted Sub-Engineer
Wood W.	1910	Sub-Engnr	Reigate	Promoted Engineer
Wood W.	1910	Stn Officer	Reigate	
Wood. W.	1911	Engineer		20 years service

Name	Year	Rank	Brigade	Other Information
Woodhouse Rbrt Edwd	1903	Fireman	Reigate	Blacksmith of Priory Road, South Park
Woodhouse A.W.	1910			Appointed reserve Fireman
Woodhouse A.	1913	Fireman		
Woodhouse A.	1913	Fireman		
Woodhouse R.	1909	Fireman	Reigate	
Woodhouse R.	1913	Sub-off.		
Woodhouse R.	1910	Fireman	Reigate	
Woodhouse ST.	1910	Fireman	South Park	Appointed to reserve
Woodhouse ST.	1911	Fireman	South Park	Replaced Laker (deceased)
*Woodhouse S.	1912	Fireman	South Park	Killed in action 6th July 1917 buried Poperinge West Vlaaderen Belgium
Woodman W.	1909	Fireman	Reigate	
Woodman E.	1900	Fireman	Earlswood	Appointed in place of of Wm Walker
Woodman E.	1910	Fireman		Resigned
Worsfold, Edmund	18/12/1899		Redhill	Promoted to Sub-Engineer
Worsfold, Edmund	1903	Sub-eng	Redhill	Promoted to Engineer
Worsfold, Edmund	1909	Eng	Redhill	Retired by age - made Hon. Fireman

ODE TO A LENGTH OF OLD HOSE

Worn and cast, done for at last,
Thy day is gone, thy time has passed;
Condemned Hose, thy die is cast.
For forty years thou has been tried
By sturdy firemen, side by side,
Seeking out the post of danger.
To sturdy hands thou art no stranger,
While rushing through thee a saving stream
Destroyed the fearful red fire's gleam;
Thou erst wert strong, no leakage there,
Thou would'st any amount of pressure bear;
But, like old men with port-wine gout,
Tho' sound to look at, thou'st worn quite out.
And, as to Hose we cannot give a pension,
Thy virtues here have 'honourable mention.'
And, dear old friend, oft as we met together,
At drills, or fires, you never shew'd white feather.

M., *1st March 1881*

Bibliography and Sources

Minutes of Reigate Borough Council meetings

'Memories of Yesterday', by Alan Ingram

'Reigate Through the Ages', by Wilfred Hooper

'A Short History of the Reigate Borough Fire Brigade', by A/Sub-Officer F. Legg

'Fire-marks' by John Vince, 1973, published by Shire Publications

Vigiles, the magazine of the Surrey Fire Preservation Trust

Fire Brigade record books (private collection)

Vestry records 1790-1920

Reigate Borough Churchwardens Accounts 1788-1858

Reigate Borough Council Minutes, 1863-1941

Chief Constable's reports to the Reigate Watch Committee for various years

Chief Fire officer's reports to the Reigate Watch Committee for various years

Reigate Borough Watch Committee Minutes 1864-1913, 1939-1945

History of Surrey by Manning and Bray

Jack Moore, his autobiography (private collection)

Acknowledgments

In the course of researching and writing this history contact was been made with a great number of very interesting and helpful people. Grateful thanks are extended for their invaluable assistance.

Jack Bish
'Fire' magazine (A national publication published from offices in Redhill)
The Holmesdale Natural and Local History Museum
Janet Jordan (Sutton Coldfield)
Evelyn Knight
Mrs Evelyn Legg
George Lucas
Fred Sherrington Legg
Mrs Martin
Jack Moore
Paul Oakford
Redhill Library
Reigate and Banstead Borough Council
Ron Shettle
The Fire Brigades of Surrey Preservation Trust
The Surrey Mirror
Mrs Marie Walton
Les Warne
Bob Sims - photo of Redhill Fire Brigade outside The Market Hall
Keith Harding
Ron Oram

And to anyone omitted, profuse apologies and multiple thanks.